Alzheimer's

Shadow

Families Facing Critical Decisions

Mitchell L. Gelber, Ed.D.

ISBN: 0988628201
ISBN-13: 9780988628205

Dedication

Throughout this book, I have drawn from those who have been affected by the ravages of Alzheimer's disease. This book is dedicated to the millions who have spent countless hours providing their devotion and care to their affected loved ones. I am humbled by the families and their tireless commitment, strength and sheer determination.

To those of you who work with people afflicted with Alzheimer's disease and their families, thank you. Thanks Dad, early playmate, coach and mentor. You worked hard and took care of EVERYONE in our extended family. Mom, you gave to Dad the care no one else ever could and continued with your grandchildren and great grandchildren.

My mind, now disengaged from my body where it was once firmly attached, floats, as a feather blown by the wind with no guiding map

M. Gelber

Acknowledgments

Thank you to the physicians, social workers, nurses and support staff that I work with, learn from and who challenge me to work at a high level; your dedication and patience are limitless. You have shown what true care-giving is.

Candace, your editing and organization gave this manuscript '*bookness*'. To Meg, Sam and Jeff, your comments were very helpful and gave me fresh exciting perspectives. Jeff, your knowledge in prescribing medications to work WITH patients and respect their humanness is inspiring. Natalie, thank you for bringing your artistic gifts to help with the cover design of this manuscript. Breakfast boys, thanks for caring for Mitchell through this process. Bon, you are my inspiration; *even though!* Oh, and Tuula, wake up this is really important.

Table of Contents

Dedication iii

Acknowledgments v

Introduction ix

Chapter One: Alzheimer's Dementia: Early Phase 1
   Overview.. 1
   Family Considerations...................................... 3
   Changes in Cognition.. 6
   Accommodations for Care 7
   Supporting Cases 15

Chapter Two: Alzheimer's Dementia: Moderate Phase 69
   Overview..69
   Family Considerations...................................... 72
   Changes in Cognition.. 80
   Accommodations for Care 82
   Supporting Cases 90

Chapter Three: Alzheimer's Dementia: Advanced Phase 127
   Overview.. 127
   Family Considerations...................................... 133
   Accommodations for Care 136
   Supporting Cases 143

Chapter Four: Dementia 177
    Dementia and the Brain... 177
    About the Dementias.. 181
    When Alzheimer's Disease Is Suspected 192
    The Diagnosis: Through the Phases............................. 199

Chapter Five: Further Considerations 207
    Closing.. 207
    References... 235

Introduction

"Imagine your brain as the hard drive of your not-so-new computer and it's suddenly become damaged for no apparent reason. Now imagine all your most recently saved files being deleted first, inexplicably. They are irretrievable. The destruction continues with slow and unrelenting erasure of word files, music, and photos you had stored from previous months and years, with the deletion continuing unabated until there is almost nothing much left and the computer is almost inoperable.

Now imagine that you go to see someone about fixing your damaged computer and all he has are jumper cables, a hammer, and a screwdriver."

John Hopkins Medicine,
The John Hopkins Bulletins
Memory Disorders, Spring 2011,
Paul B. Rosenberg, M.D.

DEMENTIA: This is *the* silent dread for people who have had a parent or grandparent diagnosed with Alzheimer's disease. A change in memory or clear thinking raises suspicion and worry of having some sort of *'family gift'*. Statistically, the older you live, the greater is the chance that you will end up with some form of dementia, most likely Alzheimer's disease. This book addresses the progressive changes that Alzheimer's disease causes in the person with the disease, in the family, and in others intimately involved in care.

At this writing (2012), there are approximately 10.9 million who are in care-giving positions with people in the grip of Alzheimer's disease, the debilitating killer of an estimated 5.4 million (and growing) people each year. Family members provide more than 17 billion hours of unpaid care, valued at $202.6 billion, according to latest figures from the Alzheimer's Association. Multiply that number by 3, 4, or 5 and that comes close to those affected by the disease in some personal way. Alzheimer's disease is the sixth leading cause of death in the United States, at a cost of $183 billion per year (Rabins Spring 2012). There is no cure, there is no reversing the course, and there is no shying away from the obvious truth: Alzheimer's is a family disease where one family member will die. The statistics mentioned above will change. With no known cure in sight, the impact of Alzheimer's disease will continue grow and play a major factor in family planning. In this book I include as family all who are in continuing contact with those afflicted and who provide some kind of care that supports health, safety, and nurturing during the disease process. I am not in a position to measure "care"—you are, and you know by your own standards whether you are "family." Suffice it to say that the family understands how much time, effort, and physical and mental anguish, and joy can be involved in caring for those with this killer disease.

People who are thinking clearly are able to problem-solve independently, learn new information, retain the information, and perform self-care with independence. They function best when operating with a familiar schedule, when they can make independent choices as appropriate, and have time to learn new and complex tasks with reduced background interference. Being deprived of personal independence is a powerful loss; it means losing capabilities that healthier people take for granted. Driving a car, selecting items at the grocery store or clothes for the day—such simple choices as these become challenging and eventually are lost for a person with dementia. The flip side of losing independence is the increase in *dependence* on others, most notably the family.

Early in the disease process I may get lost driving in areas vaguely familiar to me and get stressed in high-stimulation situations. With moderate Alzheimer's, if I am still driving, I will get lost driving in familiar places, not know how to get home from the market, and become dangerous on the road. With advanced Alzheimer's I will lose understanding of the use of a car. These types of changes hold important indications for how family members respond, the level of independence remaining for the person, and general implications for outside interventions and treatments.

Patterns in families are established early, when a marriage is new and children are young. Communication, identified roles, and accepted norms define how members of the family work, play, and nurture one another. These are life-long patterns that repeat with little change regardless of time and age. Most adult children, when returning to their parents' home with their own children, will have moments when they *accept* the child role in front of their children. When a senior family member develops dementia and can no longer function at the previous cognitive level, role changes occur that challenge others in the family to adjust their established ways. These role changes, in turn, produce conflicts within the family system. The increased loss of independence of the person with Alzheimer's creates growing dependence on family members providing direct care. The "role reversal" puts added stress on the entire system and confuses younger children when their parents begin "parenting" the children's grandparents.

Another change that occurs is that of *alliance.* The ways we connect with our family at primary levels—how we socialize, make pacts, and share information—are constructed by the development of values and morals formed as children. The progressive cognitive limitations caused by the disease begin to erase established alliances formed by families and through friendships as the person with Alzheimer's misinterprets and distorts information while forgetting the connections to significant others.

In 2012, for the first time in 27 years new criteria and guidelines for the diagnosis of Alzheimer's disease have been published. These changes have been led jointly by workgroups from the National Alzheimer's Association and the National Institutes of Health. Two of the key changes are the creation of specific phases or stages of Alzheimer's disease and the inclusion of **biomarkers**.

The first phase of Alzheimer's (the guidelines referenced above use the term "stages" instead of "phases") is now called **preclinical Alzheimer's disease**. Professionals agree that people can have a long period during which changes are occurring in the brain but no outward symptoms are displayed. The outcome of research into this phase is the ability to predict who is at highest risk for developing the disease and ultimately prevent Alzheimer's. As described above, biomarkers may eventually aid in identifying this phase.

The second phase is now called **mild cognitive impairment (MCI) due to Alzheimer's disease**. This phase is marked by mild changes in memory and thinking ability. These changes are evident to the affected loved one or close family and friends, but not severe enough to interfere with daily activities. It is believed that everyone who develops Alzheimer's dementia will have a period of MCI, and not everyone who develops MCI will develop Alzheimer's dementia. MCI can be caused by several other factors, such as reactions to medications, depression, vitamin deficiency, Parkinson's disease, or a brain trauma.

The third phase is **dementia due to Alzheimer's disease**. This phase, marked by changes in memory or cognitive abilities and behavior that impair an individual's daily life, is currently the most commonly diagnosed and what the general public perceives as Alzheimer's disease.

The focus of this book will be phases two and three, according to the nomenclature used in the new guidelines: mild cognitive impairment and dementia due to Alzheimer's disease. It is during these phases that the family becomes intimately affected and remains so through the course of the disease.

This book is set up into distinct segments: In Chapters 1, 2, and 3, I describe the progression of the disease in three overlapping phases (early, moderate, and advanced). Each phase is introduced with an *Overview Section* to acquaint the reader with the most significant features of the phase and how the progression of the disease affects the identified person **and** family. *Global concerns* will be addressed in each phase's overview section. They include: safety, flow of communication, attention to legal, medical, and social concerns, development of long-term plans, the challenge of change, grief, and guilt.

This is followed by a section depicting typical cases families may encounter, with author feedback and suggestions for care. Additionally, at the conclusion of the author comments for each case, there is a space for the reader to think and write about how this case is similar to or different from the reader's own story. The cases attempt to capture the *tone* of the changes that are occurring in the affected individual. Although situations vary from day to day or family to family, there are common signs and symptoms that appear throughout the course of the disease. After each chapter's cases, there is a reader participation form to assist families with their plans.

Some readers may choose to read the individual cases in each phase prior to reading the overview for that phase. Whichever format you choose, I am certain you will gain important insight and information to assist you.

Chapter 4 is included for those readers who would like more technical and medical information regarding the basic etiology and manifestations of Alzheimer's disease and looks at other forms of dementia that parallel and conflict. The final chapter will serve to assimilate and summarize previous information, assist with providing a timeline to help identify the myriad changes and simplify an action plan, and focus on key concepts and trends for the family. In the text, you will see author names and years—for example (Gelber 1999). These will guide you to works in the bibliography where you can find more information about the subject at hand.

I will provide an in-depth presentation of the phases of Alzheimer's disease as noted above, defining each by means of clear cognitive and behavior changes, most of which are readily identifiable to family members and others intimate with the affected person. Symptoms within each phase are experienced with varying intensity and progressively increase over time.

The road map of Alzheimer's disease is not all downhill. Yes, the outcome is known, the person afflicted will die, AND the road definitely has high points that reflect the discoveries, rediscoveries, and general outpouring of love and nurturing that can occur in families faced with the restrictions the disease presents for us. The mural has many colors and many sides. As John Zeisel, Ph.D., states in his sensitive book *I'm Still Here*, "The skills and capacities of people living with Alzheimer's that don't diminish over time, or do so more slowly, provide windows for connections and communication. Through those windows lie opportunities to establish and build new and vibrant relationships that can sustain us and them over time, supporting both care and well-being." As the disease progresses (dementias in general, Alzheimer's specifically), there are numerous changes affecting each family member, the family system, and the larger picture involving the professional community and care interventions.

My sincere hope is that you are able to use this book as a stimulus to develop your own effective personal plan. Aim to maintain the integrity of the person affected with Alzheimer's, while providing the love, understanding, and care that you and all family members deserve.

Chapter 1

Alzheimer's Dementia: Early Phase

"…Mrs. Kakugawa," he continues.
"You're walking down the street and you find a letter.
It has an address and a stamp on
Tell me what you will do with this letter"
Once again my genius in disguise answer,
"I'll check the address and deliver it to the house."

Of course she will. She knows all the neighbors.
Another great step for her brain cells.

Wrong. He marks negative on her chart.
"Increase her Aricept…"

Moon Mosaic: Caregiving Through Poetry
Easing The burden Of Alzheimer's Disease
Diagnosis: Genius Rejected
Francis H. Kakugawa, 2002

Segment One:
Overview

Looking back on how dementia affects a family, it often becomes apparent that signs were denied, minimized, and missed at each point of the disease. The reader will discover this is extremely common. When families are involved with AD, it is very difficult to see the subtle changes as they occur, and when the changes *are* noticed in the individual, there is a tendency to view them as exceptional, not the norm. Because many of the early symptoms are subtle and *common* in other people of age (most prominently forgetfulness), there is a tendency to not scrutinize them in the same way one would, for example, a large growth on the arm, or a rash across the back, or blood in the urine. As the changes *are* accepted, they are noticed as a group of symptoms, which are easier to distinguish as a growing problem. Cognitive slips are part of everyone's life and generally exposed with laughter and teasing. Most adult children do not spend daily time with their parent(s) and are not privy to the ongoing and maybe not-so-subtle changes taking place. People with mild cognitive impairment and early Alzheimer's dementia are functional, productive, social individuals who, over time during the latter part of the early phase, begin to show apparent and consistent signs of the disease. It is not until others notice or comment on these changes that we begin to take notice, gather the tales, and think about taking action.

Mentioning evidence of change to the affected person is often difficult. It may cause embarrassment that others are noticing cognitive and behavioral oddities and errors. If the person has gained some insight to the changes, the level of fear and denial have already been at work and could exacerbate already existing symptoms when brought to the forefront. There is also the possibility that the affected loved one will become increasingly secretive about and hide new or escalating changes.

If the person with Alzheimer's is living alone or with a spouse, other family members are probably not hearing about or observing the changes that are taking place. Because there does not appear to be a consistent decline in the cognitive presentation, family members may naively support the denial and minimizing. Caregiver time at this point is low but is slowly becoming more of a factor in the intimate relationships with the affected loved one. The "*sleight of mind*" factor, or the ability to "fake good," is taking hold of the family. It is essential that, at sometime soon after you and others notice common changes in the person with Alzheimer's, you make contacts with professionals who can accurately diagnose the concerns and provide a concrete helpful course of action. Keep regularly scheduled appointments with physicians, if possible, notifying them in advance of the particular concerns you have regarding what you're observing or hearing about. If changes in routine or medication are necessary, it is best if the affected loved one hears this coming from a professional, to lower the denial and minimizing of the symptoms or safety issues involved.

Segment Two:
Family Considerations

As families delve into this realm of the unknown, there are obvious and subtle ways by which we learn to cope prior to the full acceptance of the devastation and humiliating effects of dementia. Two of the most common *strategies* that help to temporarily protect and ease our way into planning and acceptance are **denial** and **minimization.**

Denial: Denial is a protection for feeling helpless, fearful, or pained about a situation that hinders our taking action. Denial of difficult change is common, and often quite helpful for temporary coping. Denial can help people get through initial shock, grief, and crises by providing *time* for the slow acceptance of the event. If denial continues and movement to regain personal strength is hampered, the translation may be an increase in depressive and anxiety symptoms, loss of caring for self and poor safety awareness for the affected person.

It's easy to deny recognition of Alzheimer's symptoms, because cognitive and behavioral changes can be experienced for any number of medical or psychiatric reasons. Furthermore, family members may describe changes as "age-related" and "normal." A major problem with this thinking, of course, is the potential danger of missing signs that may slow and/or postpone actions that family or professionals could/would take. These tendencies may put the person with Alzheimer's in greater risk situations, particularly those who live alone. If the adult child of a person with Alzheimer's lives far away, having neighbors share information about Mom on the telephone may help overcome resistance to the truth about her decline.

Minimization: There is a freshly baked apple pie on the counter. The aroma is powerful, and the sign says "free slice." Most people will justify their desire for that slice of freshly baked pie by convincing themselves that they have somehow earned a slice or by thinking of the "minimal" effect it will have on the waistline, especially after a hearty workout.

In the same way, people can make less of their lapses of memory. It is *no big deal* that I left the stove on yesterday or that I made a $100 mistake in my checkbook and overdrew my account....three times in the last two weeks—**"Everybody makes mistakes!"** Related memory concerns are one of the classic early signs of AD and countless other medical and mental health problems. The fear associated with memory decline in a family member can be extreme. I have experienced in my practice family members who will attend an assessment with a loved one suspected of cognitive impairment and interrupt the meeting with reasons why the client does not answer a question correctly—or even minimize the importance of the question itself! Initially, I may be uncertain if the family member is attempting to protect the client from facing such impairments or protecting themselves from accepting the changes.

During this time, there are several common ways to provide accommodation and safety to the affected loved one without raising alarms. These include:

- Offer more time to complete tasks rather than taking them over.
- Ask what kind of assistance would be most helpful if needed. An open-ended question may be too difficult for the affected loved one to answer. Make suggestions that he or she could follow if desired.
- Use written or verbal reminders to help the affected loved one continue with tasks (cueing).
- Make certain tasks part of a daily routine. Consistency will help with forgetfulness.
- Ask the person to gradually teach you certain tasks she or he has been performing, to ease transition tension.
- Have conversations about changes you see and give reassurance to the affected loved one's continuing role in your life.

- Take time for positive discussions to determine level of need, rather than assuming that the person with Alzheimer's can no longer perform a certain task and you need to take it over.
- Begin reminiscence activities and begin to use *anchoring* connections (these techniques will be discussed in Chapter 3).

Segment Three:
Changes in Cognition

During this phase in the disease process, there are mild, yet significant, cognitive changes that can affect and hamper personal and social functioning:

Loss of Judgment and Insight: This can result in the person with dementia making decisions that apply poor logic and displaying limited understanding of how these decisions may affect themselves and possibly others. An example could be driving a car when ability has been impaired, or maintaining a bank account and managing monthly expenses when basic adding and subtracting skills are weakened.

Impairment of Abstract Thinking: The significance of conceptual or intangible words, or of a phrase like "A bird in the hand is worth two in the bush," becomes hard to discern. Difficulties increase with explaining similarities and differences between objects and defining words and concepts that require theoretical thinking.

Aphasia: This impairment involves the loss of previously possessed abilities in language comprehension and production, resulting in an inability to understand speech. Speech abilities begin to erode; there is an increase in response time, loss of correct word use, and answers to questions become evasive. Comprehension of what others say becomes impaired and a person becomes reluctant to engage in conversation.

Apraxia: This loss of previously possessed ability to perform skilled and purposeful motor acts of a general nature is not a significant factor at this phase, although the disease begins to affect finer motor skills with detailed manipulation and sequenced procedures.

Agnosia: This is an inability to recognize objects and people. Early in this phase of the disease, the person with Alzheimer's will not display this difficulty, although there is a higher probability that the names and identifying criteria involved in recent events will be lost to memory.

Segment Four:
Accommodations for Care

As part of the overview section of each chapter, I have included several *"pay attention to"* topics that are significant indicators of change through the progression of the disease. These *Accommodations for Care* focus on important elements of care that will assist the affected loved one and care-giving family in making "best care" necessary transitions as the disease and its effects worsen. Best care varies with each family due to the myriad of demands impinging on their lives. It is significant to note that most caregivers do their best yet feel unsatisfied with their effort.

1. **Safety:** Impairments and symptoms vary in people with Alzheimer's disease. With increasing fear and denial, decision-making can become compromised, which could lead to potential self-harm and not recognizing dangers of safety in everyday life. Driving or operating machinery, care-giving others, and other situations that require immediate decisions are subject to dangerous results as the disease progresses. Safety can also be a problem in social situations when inappropriate statements or behaviors with strangers could provoke embarrassment and misunderstanding of intent.

People with mild cognitive impairment or early-phase AD perform much better with routine. Routine is important in daily life, whether traveling the same road to work or play, taking the same precautions with appliances, dialing the telephone, or using bank accounts. People pay less attention when practicing an established routine. It all sounds easy. Well, the next time you put on your jeans start with the other leg first. Did you have to stop and think a few seconds? Your mind had to adapt, maybe visualize the motions, and stick your "other" leg out first. Maybe it was not as smooth a job as usual. When routines are shifted, especially when there are multiple steps involved, confusion rises, and in situations that require making quick decisions, the results could be dangerous.

2. **Flow of communication:** Communication style—how to ask and respond to questions, when to talk and when to listen—is learned over a lifetime and flows without much thought or concern. We learn facial and body language of people close to us. People with Alzheimer's will begin to misread communications for example,. laughing at inappropriate times, or

missing the meaning of a message. This will cause more caution in interactions and affect the relationship.

Our world does not end with the family. People interact daily at the office, the club, at parties, and at school. The same basic rules of communication apply. They know us; we know them; it's a "dance" of familiarity and ease. Now suppose that one of the people in your family circle begins to behave differently. Here are a few daily life examples of when established patterns of communication breakdown or new ones develop:

- Grandma thought you said "Pick up grandson Frank after school at 3 P.M.," but you said 2 P.M. (for the fourth time in three weeks and Frank is seven years old).
- Dad calls you three times in ten minutes asking the same question.
- Your father-in-law begins misplacing tools at home and accuses you of taking them when you visit.
- Your mom rarely goes shopping to the mall: you have a joint account with her, you receive a monthly statement, and you find that Mom bought a two-thousand-dollar ring through television shopping and the new bedroom set is being delivered tomorrow.
- Wally forgets the rules of the card game you have been playing for two years and challenges the card players when someone suggests he makes a mistake.

The list of possible incidents is endless. As the disease progresses, communication patterns continue to change and become increasingly unpredictable, leading to irrevocable changes in relationships.

3. **Attention to medical, legal, and social concerns:** Forgetting scheduled appointments is common for most people due to busy schedules, emergencies, or not recording the information for later retrieval. These situations are the exceptions in our lives. **Plan ahead!** Planning and organization, for people in this phase of the disease, begins to become more difficult and confusing. Additionally, there may appear to be an increasing lethargic presentation to completing tasks necessary to run their daily lives. If a person loses their copy of the will and power of attorney and then cancels the appointment with the legal advisor because "it is not important," there is a problem! Consider that in these times, a high percentage of adult children are scattered across the United States and even the world, making it harder for them to help their parents, if necessary. There are several significant issues related to decisions of care. Notably:

- Whether the adult children are within a day's travel, or longer
- How active is the care that the adult child offers to the affected loved one
- Whether advance directives are established
- The relationship of the grandchildren who are involved with their grandparent
- Whether there is a blended family situation (which may exacerbate the conditions of the four above).

4. **Development of a long-term action plan:** The phrase "the perfect storm" comes to mind. This refers to a confluence of events that come together at once, producing outcomes that are predictable but may be disastrous. The perfect storm with Alzheimer's disease can be represented by the following variables:

- The sometimes-subtle evolution of the symptoms, with the affected loved one using a number of defense mechanisms to protect and deny any cognitive slippage
- The lack of attention given to the symptoms by people close to the person; the lack of knowledge about dementia symptoms
- The lack or slow implementation of strategies to set up a viable working plan for the family
- The lack of pre-planning regarding health checks, legal fore-planning, and financial security
- The lack of a general understanding of geriatric health, and social and life changes
- A family's plausible denial and resistance to caring for their affected loved one.

Quite a combination of events, yet all, or a large combination, is a feasible scenario.

A high percentage of middle-aged people do not set up their future with proper legal documents describing how, under what conditions, and by whom decisions are to be made for them if they are unable to do so themselves. Medical and mental health care powers of attorney, wills, and resuscitation plans defining the relevant circumstances are a few of those important decisions to be made while one is coherent and informed. When cognitive impairment becomes apparent, the decisions for the care of those with dementia are made under increased duress. The appearance of "additional caring people," the "new reality" of time limitations, and other factors can make decisions much more difficult and complicated. As the disease progresses and increasing limitations appear, not having the longer-term questions answered will interfere with emotional loss, grieving, and decision-making. People with Alzheimer's will forget or want to change what they agreed to as the disease progresses.

5. **The challenge of change:** Change occurs with the advancement of dementia. As stated earlier, the changes are subtle, minor during the earlier phase of the disease and more noticeable as the person with Alzheimer's core personality presentation alters. Maybe there is the subtle flattening of affect, or the withdrawal from challenging social situations, or inappropriate social responses. As the family begins to make adjustments due to the advancing limitations of the affected loved one, family dynamics change. Adults may be upset, tired, stressed, or simply not at home as much. Children, teens, and adults will absorb the new information differently, and a primary challenge will be helping the younger children and teens understand and learn how to assimilate the transforming situation.

6. **Grief:** Grief is a healthy phase of living that people move through when they encounter a loss with significant emotional, cognitive, behavioral, or social content. The path of grief varies. Some people begin grieving years after their loss. Take the parent whose child is lost following an unforeseen car accident. The trauma of the incident and sudden loss could keep Mom in shock and disbelief/denial for years! Adults will seek psychotherapy for moderate to severe bouts of depression, which began over the past months with no clear etiology for the symptoms. During the initial assessment, the depressed mother shares the loss of the child, months or years before, that she has never fully grieved. I have a saying:

Trauma trumps grief. When one is emotionally traumatized, grief is prolonged until there is an acceptance of the trauma itself. This can take quite a long time. Grief effects can be subtle and take many forms; sadness, fear, anger, withdrawal, and denial are the most common early emotional effects. With dementia, maybe Mom no longer finds pleasure in the once-a-week walk through the mall because it is too noisy and confusing, or Dad cannot sit through watching the Sunday football game with his daughter and grandchildren. These seemingly small changes can affect any member of the family and close friends, and they must be acknowledged.

7. **Guilt:** Family members make statements to the effect "I should have seen the signs earlier," or "If only I had paid closer attention," or "We should have moved Dad closer before this all happened." These are common responses from family members once *reality hits* and they begin to pedal uphill! In truth, most families members involved with care for the person with dementia know something has changed in their parent about one year before they seek professional intervention. Minimizing, denying, attributing changes in behavior to other causes, not paying attention, and lack of familiarity with the person's daily routine to begin with can be some of the reasons they do not act sooner. Additionally, people with Alzheimer's often find ways to explain away the "silly things" they do and say.

Mix in love and a sense of obligation to help your parent(s), and there is a tendency to blame yourself for the current situation and start your role as primary caregiver through guilt. Feeling responsible for another's life predicament, especially if there is nothing that could have been done about it in the first place, is a dangerous creed to follow. The promise of adult children to care for their parents as they get older, because of the love and caring *they* received when young, must have realistic boundaries and safety rules built in, or the grown children will be enveloped in their care-giving role to the detriment of themselves and other loved ones in their lives. Plus, as the demands of the care-giving role increase, resentment can begin to creep in and subtly sabotage the very impact of the assistance. Care-giving through guilt is an insidious, unnecessary process that has deleterious effects on the family. Caring for the loved one through a sense of obligation ("I *should* care for my parents because of all they did for me") can bring negative outcomes. Resentment concerning the increasing time and energy needed for care develops, and this resentment can consciously or unconsciously place limits on the care you offer. Other members of the family or close friends may feel a loss of closeness and support. This could result in the creation of a cycle that breeds anger and isolation, discouraging important communication and a very significant, healthy grieving process that needs to be shared within the family. Finally, the larger the dose of guilt, the less pure the grieving!

SUPPORTING CASES

The following cases present PATTERNS of signs and symptoms that are common to families with similar circumstances at this phase of the disease. Not all changes in the person with Alzheimer's can be fully attributed to the advancement of dementia. Previously existing problems caused by coexisting disease processes, environmental or social factors, or medicine reactions may cause or exacerbate the dementia symptoms.

I am presenting these cases from my practice (names and details have been changed) to help give you a sense of the scope of how the disease presents itself, and the effects it can have on family systems. Your family situation will differ from the presented cases in various ways. **At the end of each case** *presentation and discussion, you'll find space where you can consider how your family situation is like or not like that case.*

As you read the cases, consider the following action items, as a starting point to develop a plan for how you will move through the transitions that the disease brings about. You'll find space **at the end of this Supporting Cases section** *where you can plan your responses for these action points.*

- *What concrete plans must be put into motion at this time?*
- *Who will be in charge of implementing the plans?*
- *Do you require an action plan for medical, psychiatric, or legal assistance?*
- *What professionals or organizations will need to be contacted?*

- *Who will be the "Point Person" in charge of coordinating care needs with professionals and handling the unforeseen and acute situations that will arise?*
- *What support networks need to be established to provide care and education for family members?*

CASE 1 Early Phase

Carl: Husband with Alzheimer's
Robin: Wife

It is the holiday season, and the Wilburs are getting ready for their usual round of Christmas parties and get-togethers in the community. As they prepare for their first night out, Robin is finishing wrapping the cookies she baked and wondering where Carl is. Carl is sitting on the bed apparently "stuck." There are three pairs of socks on the bed next to Carl that he removed from his drawer to choose from. When questioned, he tells Robin that he was not sure which she wanted him to wear. Later, at the gathering, Robin notices how Carl is following her around the room, hovering nearby and not initiating conversations on his own. People engage him (as Carl has known a number of these people for years) but he seems distant and quiet. Carl appears to avoid talking to people he does not know and forgets their name upon introduction. Robin assumes that Carl is not feeling too well and they leave the party early. Carl takes a wrong turn on the way home and only becomes aware when Robin says something to him. It is nighttime and with him not feeling too well, he was tired, she thinks. The next day, Carl is back to his "normal" self, confirming Robin's thoughts that Carl's lapses were a one-time event.

The Wilburs have two more events (both daytime) that week, which they enjoy and celebrate with holiday cheer. The next is a Friday evening dinner event at a neighbor's home. That afternoon, when Robin reminds Carl of the dinner, he hesitates and then says he does not want to go! Robin is astounded.

17

The hosts are folks they have known for ten years. Carl gives weak excuses, and Robin jumps on all of them. They argue, and Carl finally gives in to Robin's insistence.

That weekend they are scheduled to go Christmas shopping for the grandchildren at the big mall. They have always enjoyed buying, wrapping, and sending the packages together. When Saturday comes, Carl again wants to back out, but Robin insists. Rather than having another argument, Carl quickly agrees and off they go. This is not fun. Carl is distracted and appears agitated in the crowded stores. He will not separate at all from Robin and quickly agrees to whatever she suggests they buy for the families.

Over the next several weeks, Robin begins to take special note of Carl's behaviors and routines and comes up with several discoveries. In addition to Carl having some difficulty in selecting clothes for the day, she notices that he will wear the same pants several days in a row, whether they are stained or not. There is a distinct drop-off in Carl's time with the neighbor men, and when Robin asks why he is not seeing the next door neighbor, he tells her that the neighbor is not at home and has many projects he is working on. When Robin runs into the neighbor, he asks if Carl is okay, because over the past two weeks Carl had made a number of excuses that kept them from getting together.

With the holidays over, life remains stable for the Wilburs, and Robin finds herself paying less attention to the subtle changes and requests Carl had made over the past month. Over the next several weeks Robin begins managing the household expenses, scheduling appointments for medical and social events, and, when family calls, answering the phone and doing most of the speaking. It appears easier for Robin to adjust to these new responsibilities than engage Carl on a daily basis.

Changes noted in the person with dementia and the family:

In Carl:
- Poor decision-making by Carl when given multiple choices
- Carl's growing dependency on Robin to maintain routine
- The high level of environmental stimulation increasing stress and confusion in Carl
- Carl begins to isolate himself socially
- Carl exhibits declining personal hygiene

In Robin:
- Robin's awareness of changes in Carl's behavior
- Robin's increase of responsibility for the daily routine
- Robin sets up and maintains appointments

Effects and Interventions

- Carl is having difficulty with making open-ended choices (clothes selection and choosing gifts for family) and, when pressed, becomes anxious and withdrawn. As choices mount, so does the pressure. In this case, the decline is associated with facing new situations. Reaction time to new and uncomfortable situations is slowed, and this produces a heightened anxiety. This anxiety increases the difficulty of accurate and appropriate decision-making. This produces a direction of increasing frustration and depression.

- Situations that are not part of the daily routine are becoming more difficult to manage. Problems with driving home at night, meeting new folks, and engaging in conversations with larger groups of people are keeping Carl and Robin increasingly isolated. These are common symptoms of early decline. Carl remains oriented to all facets of his life and has enough insight to know that arguing with Robin may provoke her anger, which could cause more fragility in him. Carl processes routine information properly. He is beginning to have some difficulty with retention and recent memory. Routines and scheduling events with reminders can ease any stress from memory failure or confusion. The idea of presenting lists or other forms of visual reminders at this stage is less threatening if done prior to the *formal* discussion about his growing deficits. To further reduce the possible stigma, Robin could also post her schedule.

- Carl stays close to Robin. She assumes he's not feeling well, and takes this as a reason for leaving an uncomfortable social situation. When he appears *healthier* in the morning, her *diagnosis* is confirmed. This is a common response from a spouse who may be using denial or minimizing the changes. As stated earlier in the book, denial and minimizing are useful tools for *escaping* difficult situations and can temporarily reduce the growing tension but are NOT LONG-TERM SOLUTIONS. Maintaining an active social life and facing challenging tasks will force the spouse and family to accept the changes and face up to the *no-problem-here* illusion.

- Robin is beginning the care-giving process by the subtle changes of taking on more household responsibilities and becoming the *lead* in the relationship. Again, it is common for the spouse to deny or minimize the reality of change by subtly accepting individual anomalies without looking at the larger picture of decline. If Robin does not address, for herself, the subtle alterations in their relationship, then resentment, frustration, and intimate distancing are possible outcomes. The demands of caring for Carl at this phase of the disease are minimal compared to what is in store as the disease progresses. Without Robin's full attention to and planning for the growing challenges to come, her health becomes increasingly fragile—and then, so does Carl's.

• Robin could address some of the changes she has noticed with Carl in a way that diminishes the protective/defensive posture he might have. He appears to have some self-doubt but is not sure why he has difficulties or the nature of their origin. This could allow him to begin to openly accept that *something* is happening, which could be discussed with the proper professional. Early in the first phase of the disease, as stated earlier, the affected person can be more resistant to advice and to the acceptance that something is amiss. Having a professional familiar with the situation provides bonus points for your relationship. **Professional messages are best heard from a professional.**

• Another consideration is to involve family or a person close to the family into the situation to help Robin balance her feelings and thoughts about what might be happening with Carl. Hearing a different and more objective perspective, with appropriate questions, will assist with necessary planning. Additionally, this is a time when acceptance of change is crucial to formulate an action plan. At this point, a spouse may feel emotionally *stuck* and lack initiative to get a plan going. Family and/or professionals can play a vital role in motivating healthy treatment planning.

• It is important for Carl to maintain his regularly scheduled appointments with professionals (medical, dental, and others). If Carl is missing appointments due to forgetting, or not showing up for other reasons, that should be addressed immediately. Robin would benefit from keeping a log of the changes that she notices in Carl that affect daily living, and they should be brought to the attention of their family physician or specialist. It is the professional who could best identify the *patterns of change* in the person with Alzheimer's and assist with a proper diagnosis and course of treatment. The spouse and family bring knowledge and history to the table. Combining the available resources present the best opportunity for the most complete plan.

In what ways is the above case different from or similar to your family situation?

_____

_____

_____

_____

_____

_____

CASE 2 Early Phase

Ben: Husband with Alzheimer's   Emily: Wife
Billie: Adult daughter   Keith: Son-in-Law

Ben and Emily had been living together in an assisted living situation away from the children. While driving near their residence, they were involved in a serious auto accident, leaving Ben with multiple serious injuries including a closed head trauma. Ben was placed in a rehabilitation hospital. Emily suffered minor injuries and was released back to her apartment in assisted living.

Back at home, Emily begins to become highly agitated and delusional, screaming at the staff to let her see her husband and attempting to leave. When her daughter (Billie) comes to visit and calm her, Emily accuses her daughter of trying to tear the family apart and keeping her away from her husband. She emphatically states there is nothing wrong with her, while continuing to threaten Billie. Billie is witnessing new behavior from her mom. The situation is wearing on Billie and she is beginning to show signs of increasing depression. She has good support from her husband, Keith, yet she continues to have difficulty focusing on work; she is becoming distant in her marriage relationship, with less time and energy for her children. Billie has not had a close relationship with her mother for many years and blames herself for not being able to resolve this situation and presently care for her mother.

Ben has moderate cognitive loss due to the auto accident and will remain in a skilled nursing facility for a few months. Emily remains resistive to any care and has been remanded involuntarily to an inpatient facility for a psychiatric evaluation. Following a thorough evaluation, Emily is diagnosed with dementia. It appears that Ben had been protecting Emily's cognitive decline for quite some time, and without his continued protection and presence, coupled with the auto accident and transitional living situation changes, she has declined dramatically.

Emily refuses to go into any type of residential facility. She remains steadfast that she can care for herself and wants to be with her husband to help him. She denies any difficulties and continues to accuse her daughter of trying to break up her marriage. The facility that provided the evaluation started Emily on new medications, which have eased the anxiety and confrontation. Billie has a two-week deadline to find another placement. The sudden changes in Billie's parental situation, i.e., her father's traumatic brain injury (TBI) and placement and her mother's apparent dementia, create dramatic changes, causing an upheaval in her personal and professional life.

There are several options that Billie is considering for her mother: placement in a structured facility (skilled nursing or assisted); having her mother live with Billie and her husband; or arranging for her mother to live with in-home assistance in a nearby rental Billie and her husband own. Secondary, yet just as important, is the imminent release of her father from the skilled nursing facility and what potential living arrangement changes will then be necessary.

Changes noted in the person with dementia and the family:

In Emily:
- Emily's security and routine were instantly changed by the auto accident and hospitalization of Ben

- Without her care-giving husband available, Emily becomes highly agitated, deeply confused, and accusatory
- Emily becomes highly resistant to further changes as she cannot keep up with the quantity of new adjustments
- Emily must temporarily move in with Billie and her family
- Emily continues to decline; she is remanded to an inpatient acute facility for a psychiatric evaluation and diagnosed with Alzheimer's dementia
- Emily experiences a threat to personal safety and wants to be in a familiar place, either home or with Ben
- Emily uses denial and minimization to limit the level of stress and agitation

In Ben:
- Ben has kept Emily's decline secret from their daughter
- Ben has been minimizing and denying symptoms, which builds high mutual dependence, secrecy, guilt, and fear

In Billie and her family:
- Unresolved family history begins to cause Billie misgivings
- Due to the combination of her father's TBI and mother's increased needs with the dementia, Billie's personal and professional life are in crisis.
- Secondary depression from the family situation will affect support from spouse and other family members with decreased time with children

Effects and Interventions

• Ben was Emily's anchor and, in her own way, Emily was his. Ben's *need* to not be alone and Emily's dependence on him are major contributing factors to their current dilemma. We are not sure of the degree of decline Emily experienced prior to the auto accident, but there was enough to cause a major shift in her ability to function independently on a daily basis. Sudden life changes to caregivers or anyone close to a person with dementia will cause considerable functional alterations in behavior and cognition, as routine plays an important guide to their skill maintenance. Major surprises are in store for the family members who are not privy to the daily life experiences of the affected loved one and spouse. When the spouse "awakens" following a traumatic incident like the one presented and the dramatic changes in the loved one are obvious, the most lucid of the couple can suddenly see the loss and critical situation.

• Ben's medical problems and surgery have presented a new set of concerns. Ben was the only caregiver, and aside from the confusion Emily is feeling, Ben is now faced with the reality that he cannot at this time supply the care-giving she requires. At present, we are not clear as to the longer effects of the TBI and whether he will require continuing care for himself as well. Separation from Emily has exacerbated his sense of loss. Due to Ben's medical condition, Billie has taken over primary responsibility for her mother's care and is unclear regarding the extent of her debility. It also appears that Billie will now have to prepare for the primary responsibility of her father. At this point he is properly cared for, and all attention can go to Mom, but depending on the extent of

Ben's TBI and other medical complications, he may be resistive to some of her suggested interventions.

• Emily is focusing on Ben's health. She is confused about the sudden changes and believes that Billie is the source of her separation from Ben and the turmoil in their lives. This situation has probably made it even more difficult for Emily to focus on what she requires at this point and accept her limitations. *Everything was just going so smoothly, and she wants it back.* Additionally, Emily must contend with the "reintroduction" of Billie into her life. Her present level of confusion and loss creates an increase in paranoia and protective functioning, which appears as anger and resistance to any further change. Reasoning and judgment seem to disappear.

• As revealed in the history, Billie and Emily had a contentious relationship in the past, and that seems to influence the strong current negative responses Emily has to Billie's attempt at assisting her. As stated previously, when children become adults, there are changes in the relationship that pose role shifts, and how the family adapts to these shifts will portend how the care-giving schemes will work out as the disease progresses. The level of initial compliance or resistance to care direction for the elderly is many times foreshadowed years earlier, when the elders are active parents to their children. With Ben's limited assistance during this transition and Emily's cognitive slippage, Billie will do well to have dialogs and interventions with medical and legal professionals.

• What about Billie and her new role as primary caregiver to both parents? Billie is experiencing signs of depression. An unpredictable crisis situation, where she becomes the person professionals are requesting direction from, the paranoid accusations and rage from her mother, and a history of distance and poor relationships with her mom are overwhelming. Even with the support of her husband, this is an overwhelming task. With the role change, Billie's time allotment for other parts of her life takes the brunt. Time with children and for herself disappear. Energy is depleted and focus at work is challenged.

• What next? Following stabilization of the immediate crisis, there are questions that must be addressed. These include:

* Does Emily require a secure, locked placement? The short answer is at this point in time, yes. Any transition for the person with Alzheimer's can be tenuous, and presently Emily shows no sign of being able to remain calm without medication and/or professional involvement. Whether this can be accomplished without 24/7 care is questionable. Her current level of resistance could turn violent and unpredictable.

* What role does Billie play in the coming weeks and months? This will be up to Billie. Her initial willingness to enter the fray speaks to her caring and desire to stabilize the situation. The other side, of course, is recognizing the cost to herself and her life. When do the costs outweigh the benefits? At this point, the acuity of the situation is running the show. How much and how fast will Dad (Ben) recover, and what role will he be able to play in the future care of Emily and himself?

* Should Emily be *allowed* to see Ben while he is in the hospital? Again, this is one of those questions best answered

by how Emily responds to initial treatment for herself and her ability and/or willingness to respond positively to the larger treatment plan for both of them. Will Billie have the professional support and willingness to carry through with plans that may not have the support of either parent?

* Should Billie and her husband be looking to create a living arrangement that includes Ben and Emily together, with them? At this point, it is too early to tell. I suggest the conversations begin, but there are a number of other possible living arrangements for her parents that might be more appropriate. There is the case, highly probable to unfold, wherein Emily and Ben are separated in the same environment, or in different facilities. Their needs require different treatment options and the level of care will vary.

Regardless of the decisions to come for Billie and her husband, there is no doubt that medical, legal, and mental health professional intervention is the key to future successful caregiving for themselves and treatment for her parents.

In what ways is the above case example different from or similar to your family situation?

_____

_____

_____

_____

_____

_____

CASE 3 Early Phase

Tom: Husband with Alzheimer's   Francesca: Wife
Jack: Adult son

Tom, a 79-year-old man, has recently had surgery for total left hip replacement and is currently in a rehabilitation facility. He is very confused and disoriented, with word loss and very slow processing of information. This is a dramatic change for a man who was functioning independently prior to his fall and subsequent surgery. Lingering effects of surgery and medication for pain have not been ruled out as possibly adding to his change in state of mind. Tom recognizes that he is confused and, as a result, has been fearful to proceed fully with offered therapies, not trusting himself when walking or performing daily tasks that therapists believe he can perform with more regularity. Tom is having difficulty remembering new therapy strategies that he learned the day before, with deficits noticed in concentration and in retention of any new information. When confused, Tom loses patience quickly; he denies problems, claiming he is too tired and in too much pain to continue, and asks to return to his room.

Francesca notices these changes in Tom but continues to believe that they are caused only by the surgery and medications. In attempting to deny Tom's present cognitive state and *protect* Tom from embarrassment, she has become a super caregiver. She is taking on responsibilities that Tom could and should be doing himself for therapeutic reasons, which further encourages him not to perform and recover physically, to continue to doubt himself, and possibly to develop a depressive state. She begins to finish his sentences when he loses a word and make jokes about his "silly mistakes." This angers Tom, and they begin to argue.

Jack, one of their adult sons is coming to visit Tom in the hospital and does not know of the changes that have taken place in Tom's thinking processes since the surgery. Francesca picks her son up at the airport and "prepares" him before meeting his dad. In her preparation, she encourages Jack to "take it easy" on his father and have patience with his confusion, as "he is going through a rough time, but I expect him to recover fully." Jack enters the room and Dad says "Paul, what are you doing here?" Dad forgets the specific nature of his medical condition and says that he hurt his leg and they are fixing him up. He is vague about the implications on his daily functioning.

Outside the room, Jack tells the doctor that he witnessed a decline in his dad over the past year and had mentioned this to his mother. He states that he has been talking much less on the telephone, not speaking to the grandchildren, and he has been vague about his daily life. Jack's mom disagrees, providing excuses for Tom's change and saying this is all about the surgery and pain medication.

With Tom's diminished work in therapies, the facility must discharge him elsewhere. Francesca hints strongly that with in-home assistance, she can care for Tom at home. Jack voices his concerns about the toll that would take on his mother and the limited rehabilitation his dad would receive. The doctor urges Francesca to have Tom temporarily placed in a more structured environment to see if he regains more of his cognitive and functional ability. Tom wants to go home; he is adamant that he will succeed with in-home care and assistance from his wife.

Changes noted in the person with dementia and the family:

In Tom:
- Medical conditions, especially those involving acute changes in functioning or medications that alter cognitive functioning, setting off a reaction that exacerbates the pace of the disease
- Confusion with disorientation to time and place
- Processing directions and requests slowly
- Difficulty learning new skills necessary to proceed with rehabilitation
- Denial and substitution (fatigue) as a reason for difficulty in picking up on the requested learning techniques
- Loss of tolerance and increase of agitation with difficulty in following directions and learning new tasks
- Increased anger at Francesca when she interjects or does not let him finish his communication
- Confusion and memory disorientation for current medical concerns

In Francesca:
- Using denial and continuing to blame the cognitive difficulties on the recent surgery and medications
- Becoming the *super caregiver:* providing care for Tom and thereby having him not challenge his deficiencies
- Making excuses and jokes about the *silly mistakes* Tom makes in therapies
- Finishing statements or answering Tom's questions before he can finish expressing his thoughts

- Encouraging their son to minimize the changes he may notice in his father, stating that they are only temporary

In Jack (son):
- Refusing to keep the secret; reporting to the medical doctor that his dad has shown signs of change prior to the hip fracture

Effects and Interventions

- The effects of the anesthesia have worn off, and yet Francesca clings to the notion that Tom's cognitive decline is temporary and will correct itself. This will not happen. Francesca passively *supports* the notion that Tom does not have to participate in therapies by not accepting the permanency of the changes and offering excuses. Again, the role of denial and minimization come into play and may hinder the progress Tom can make with therapies.

- With Tom's denial of problems and Francesca's complicity, Tom has medical conditions that are not being addressed. This will lead to him leaving the facility and possibly facing increased physical problems in the future. Francesca must face or have help in facing her own emotions about what is happening; then she can help Tom alleviate his fears and they can work together to move forward. Tom will not willingly move to a placement other than his own home. The probability of Tom succeeding at home, from a cognitive perspective, is good. With the right medication, professional intervention, and training for Francesca, Tom could continue to have quality safe time at home.

• Francesca is attempting to become Tom's spokesperson, a role common with spouses who face the *loss* of their loved one. This is not healthy on several fronts: If Tom does not challenge himself cognitively, he will become increasingly passive and dependent on Francesca to provide more and more for him. Francesca will *willingly* take on that role to "help" her husband, slowly sinking into the full-time caregiver role; this will further facilitate the loss of the spousal, lover role, and as Francesca assumes more and more responsibility for Tom's life, they will begin to isolate themselves from others and potential support networks. Additionally, as stated above, Francesca must let Tom fully recover physically.

• Jack can play a vital role in helping his parents move through this transition period, if his mom allows him to. If Francesca continues in her attempt to *control* the outcome, she runs the possibility of alienating Jack. If their rift becomes the center of attention, then Tom loses out on their joint support, planning, and care. At present, there are no indications of what role Jack may want in his folks' life. Considering he came to the rehabilitation hospital to see his dad, their communication must be at least satisfactory. The amount of time and level of input from Jack will play an important role as the disease progresses. Will Francesca accept Jack's input?

• The rehabilitation facility placement is temporary, and Francesca must decide what kind of placement would best suit Tom at this stage of rehabilitation in light of the continuing cognitive changes. The options include Tom returning home, with in-home daily care, or admitting Tom to an assisted or skilled nursing care facility to continue a more structured therapy program. Jack expresses deep concern for the safety and therapy care his dad would receive if he went directly home. He does not believe that Dad could receive the best care due to Mom's position of protection coupled with Dad's apparent losses. Tom is adamant that he is quite capable of succeeding at home. He states that Francesca can take better care of him than anyone else. The stage is set for a difficult period with much stress and family discord. When one considers the reasoning for each member of the family, each of their positions appears *right*. Jack's opinion at this time is probably no match to counter Francesca's denial, or Tom's level of functionality and strength of desire to return home. Jack's move may be to support his parents with Tom's return home and push hard for strong in-home care along with professional training and counseling for his mother.

In what ways is the above case different from or similar to your family situation?

_____

_____

_____

_____

_____

_____

CASE 4 Early Phase

Sam: Husband with Alzheimer's   Lucille: Wife
Caitlyn: Adult daughter   Janae: Adult daughter

Sam and Lucille have been married 56 years. They live in a small house in a working-class neighborhood. Both have been retired several years from their long-time county jobs. Sam was in the military and now volunteers at the Veterans Administration and works part-time at a local discount chain as a food taster. Lucille stays at home, plays canasta once a week with friends, and walks daily with her dog. She generally prepares dinner nightly and manages daily chores.

They have two children. Their daughter Caitlyn and her family live two blocks north, and they see the grandchildren regularly. Sunday is barbeque day at the grandparents', with Sam grilling the food. Everyone laughed the time Sam forgot to turn on the gas and let the food "cook" at a low heat for an hour, checked it, and then discovered he did not ignite the burner; or the time he left the food in the car overnight in July and the meat spoiled; or when he went to work a day earlier than scheduled. No one laughed the second time he did that!

Their other daughter, Janae, lives downstate with her family, and they visit with Sam and Lucille monthly. They have not noticed the odd behaviors but have commented on Sam's mood changes, especially with their elementary-age children. Sam always played with them whenever they came to visit. They would go outdoors and kick the soccer ball or spend time playing video games. When the four young grandchildren are together, there is much noise and activity, with the children running through the house playing make believe and leaving their toys all about. Increasingly, Sam has become more distant, going to his bedroom to "take a nap" while the families are visiting. Sam finds ways to *escape* talking on the telephone with both families.

Sam has always had a temper, but over the past few months his anger has gotten out of hand. Several times recently, while arguing, he has gotten nose to nose with Lucille and even pushed her and stormed out of the house. The next day, he denied touching Lucille and blamed their argument on her. He could not recall the details of the situation. Lucille has not shared any of the changes she has observed, or the violence shown by Sam, with her daughters. She is considering talking to a professional but not sure whom to approach.

Recently, she came home from a hike with a friend and Sam was seemingly poring over their bank statements. He angrily rose from the table and asserted that Lucille had withdrawn three thousand dollars from their checking account five days earlier, claiming that she had taken the money out without his knowledge. Lucille knew that they had major landscaping completed two weeks prior, but Sam had forgotten. When he calmed down, Lucille showed Sam the receipt and suggested that he had forgotten that the cost was so much.

On a daily basis, Sam is able to function with regularity, attending to simple tasks. Sam performs the routine chores (taking out the garbage, setting the table, making the bed), but when something out of the ordinary or unexpected requires attention, Lucille *assigns* the task to Sam. He does not pick up on change very well. Last weekend they went to the local mall and bought a hammock that required assembly. Lucille wanted to have the teen next door assemble it, but Sam protested loudly, stating that Lucille was treating him like a child. Two hours later, with parts strewn over the lawn, Sam came in, slammed the screen door, and went to their bedroom, not to be seen for the rest of the afternoon. Lucille did not raise the issue and it was never talked about.

Changes noted in the person with dementia and the family:

In Sam:
- Recent memory lapses—forgetting to bring food into the house, not turning the grill on
- Going to volunteer on the wrong day
- Isolating from the younger children and families when they visit
- Increased mood changes with greater anger—pushing his wife
- Blaming disagreements on the other person
- Difficulty learning new information
- Difficulty with multitasking and completion of tasks having sequential steps
- Apparently requiring cuing from Lucille to think of and complete some chores

In Lucille:
- Not letting their daughters know of the escalated anger episodes
- Apparently avoiding discussions with Sam about his cognitive slippage

- Not getting around to consulting any professionals regarding the cognitive and behavior changes noted in Sam
- Not addressing the changes in the relationship between Sam and their grandchildren

Effects and Interventions

- Sam is having difficulty with recent recall and, because he is questioning himself and others more without clear memory, his level of agitation is increased. This in turn increases suspiciousness and caution. He is withdrawing from family time. There could be several reasons for this: wishing to "protect" himself from others; feeling frightened and ashamed about sharing his self-observations; falling into a depressive state; becoming more suspicious about those around him; or some combination of those factors. It appears that the family has used humor to deal with past concerns, and this pattern could be used to avoid facing the emotional turmoil ahead.

- Lucille has not shared any of her concerns or the observed changes in Sam with anyone. Why? This is not a good idea for several reasons. Most important are the safety factors; Sam's level of daily functioning appears to be stable at this moment, but that could change without warning, at which time he may need medical or psychological intervention. Also, Lucille is putting herself in questionable safety, considering that Sam has already assaulted her and denied or forgotten the incident. Sam is growing increasingly suspicious through his forgetfulness and confusion and has questioned her about "missing" money. She is attempting to handle this single-handedly, without any support from family or friends. Also to consider is that Lucille's behavior and response to Sam will change as she becomes frustrated and less tolerant of his verbal and behavioral changes, which will, in turn, impact his response style and increase his suspiciousness and agitation: a vicious cycle indeed!

• Sam had forgotten that they had landscaping and then accused Lucille of stealing $3,000 that was used to finance the work. There may be other situations where Sam could not clearly identify cause and effect that would arouse his suspiciousness and lead to arguments and accusations. A number of the noted "errors" Sam has made appear to be connected to *learning in steps*; that is, completion of non-routine activities that require a series of steps to complete (using the grill, putting the hammock together, playing video games with grandchildren). When Sam is confused or forgetful he challenges Lucille or withdraws from any social contact. Lucille needs to find a confidant immediately, someone she could speak with openly about what has already transpired, who could help her raise questions to appropriate professionals. Groundwork needs to be set concerning how a support system will proceed.

• Lucille has questioned herself as to whether she should seek professional consultation, and the answer is emphatically yes. I would approach a medical physician first and proceed from there. A medical physician knowledgeable about geriatric medical conditions would be helpful in determining the causes for the notable changes in Sam. There may be several alternative reasons for his changes in behavior and cognition. If the evaluation points in the direction of dementia or another psychiatric disorder, an evaluation by a mental health specialist with knowledge of gerontology is warranted. Legal (consider advanced directives) and financial plans by an elder law specialist must be updated and tailored to meet the changing needs of the situation. Sam will become less amenable and able to participate in following a logical and helpful plan. His appropriate input is time limited.

• Speaking to the family will give Lucille's children and grandchildren a chance to address any "weird" behavior they have noticed and begin to provide a basic knowledge base for helping the children adjust. As stated in other sections of the book (Chapter I overview and Chapter 5), younger children require clear, concrete understanding to help them *tie their thoughts together and make sense on their thinking levels.* Children and teens have an enhanced ability to adjust to changing situations with the proper knowledge, support, and role modeling from their parents. The longer Lucille or her children do not address the noticed changes in Sam, the greater the difficulty becomes in formulating a viable plan and the greater the possibility the grandchildren will shy away.

• There may be reason to believe that other family members or friends have noticed changes in Sam and Lucille but have refrained from approaching either of them. This may be an established family dynamic that requires attention sooner rather than later. It is all too easy to repeat familiar patterns of communication during high stress times and, conversely, much more difficult to change established behaviors during high stress times. As stated earlier, family patterns tend to repeat themselves, especially during crises, and old familiar roles appear with norms about communication, reliance, and trust. If one or both of Sam and Lucille's children want to withdraw from any active participation in the planning or care for either parent, it is best to openly discuss this and plot a course based on the information at this point. As the disease progresses and Lucille unexpectedly finds herself without the pledged family support, it may have a severe effect on her personal health and ability to assist with Sam's level of care.

In what ways is the above case different from or similar to your family situation?

_____

_____

_____

_____

_____

_____

CASE 5 Early Phase

Nancy: Mother with Alzheimer's
Gregg: Deceased husband
Katherine: Adult daughter (oldest)   Milt: Adult son
Abby: Adult daughter (youngest)

Gregg and Nancy lived in a small town in the southwest. They were married for 49 years. Recently, Gregg had a massive stroke and died. While this was somewhat unexpected, Gregg had a history of medical problems and in earlier days was a daily alcohol and cigarette user. As a dad, he was seen as distant and emotionally unavailable to his three children, who are scattered about the United States. Nancy now lives by herself in their home.

Nancy's relationship with her children has been stormy for many years. She was reportedly verbally abusive to her children and unavailable for emotional support while they were growing up. She drank with less regularity than Gregg, had better physical health, and now appears very resentful of his death. The adult children have found it prudent to have little contact with their parents in the past 15 years. Their dad's death has changed the situation. Since Gregg's death, Nancy has found reasons to call each of the children on an almost daily basis. The three children have also begun talking daily, and through their sharing of information they find they have conflicting stories from their mother concerning her daily functioning and general state of thought clarity. She is telling each child different stories about her day with poor memory recollection of contacts with local people. The children decide that one of them must go to visit their mother and clearly discover what her true situation is like. The three children were not very close growing up with the lack of central support from their parents; they did not spend much time together while in the same household, nor have they since adulthood. They went their separate ways to establish their own lives. Attending their dad's funeral was the first direct contact the three had together in four years.

The oldest daughter, Catherine, lives in Kansas City. Catherine is angry about this turn of events. She does not want close contact with her mother and would rather stay connected, and manage the situation, from long distance.

Milt, the middle child, lives by himself in Oregon. He is semi-retired and has been the most passive of the three, with very limited contact with other family members. The closest to him appears to be the younger sister, Abby, whom he has seen twice over the past several years.

Abby and her partner live in Maine. She would like to be more involved with this situation but feels a financial pinch that inhibits her hands-on involvement.

Following several telephone conversations, the three children decide that Milt will visit with Mom, assess the situation, and take the lead in preparing whatever plans need to be put in place. Milt discovers that Mom can be functionally appropriate on a daily basis, following a routine for daily care, preparing light meals, and completing basic household-related activities. But Milt discovers that she is unable to keep track of details in her life. She has pill bottles open on the counter, legal documents strewn on the dining room table, and a large pile of laundry near the washing machine. Mom is lucid most times but cannot answer questions about bill paying or scheduled appointments. She refuses to leave home, and even though she enjoys the company of her son, she has moments of nasty verbal comments and questioning why he is at her home. Several nights, he awakens to find his mom puttering in the kitchen. She is moving contents of one cabinet to another and back again. Milt questions her behavior and she becomes verbally nasty and unable to supply satisfactory answers. Milt sets up appointments with her family physician who refers her to a psychologist for an evaluation of her mental status. They determine that Nancy has mild dementia.

With new medication and the recommendation that she not live by herself, Milt takes the lead in finding placement for Mom. Milt's visit is temporary, and so arrangements must be made quickly. This poses several concerns regarding placement and decision-making responsibilities. Mom is resistant to leaving her home and cannot understand the importance and number of tasks necessary for any type of transition.

Changes noted in the person with dementia and the family:

In Nancy:
- Poor recall and distortion of facts
- Poor attention to details
- Inability to keep track of important documents
- Poor personal hygiene
- Not tracking medication use
- Moments of confusion and disorientation
- Declining judgment and insight

- Isolation and fear of leaving home
- Change in sleep habits

In the adult children:
- As a group, must decide in a limited amount of time,
  o what the options are
  o who is going to take the lead
  o what role each may play in this transition and continuing saga
- May exhibit resistance to become involved with *family* matters at this point in their lives
- Find themselves balancing family history with current affairs

Effects and Interventions

• Nancy has periods of confusion with difficulty in retention of recent information, poor attention to detail, and poor judgment and reasoning. With the history of little closeness in the family over the past 15 years, Nancy's sudden increase in communication with her children seem to indicate that she is aware there has been some change in *her* daily functioning. Whether Gregg's death precipitated her changes is questionable, but likely, given the dramatic personal loss. Could their relationship have been dependent, with them protecting and supporting each other enough to function without alarm, or could the loss itself have produced a substantial emotional turmoil to trigger the cognitive decline?

• Nancy continues to *stay busy*, but with little accomplishment of task: incomplete laundry, paperwork, kitchen cabinet transfers; she appears unable to handle financial responsibilities. Telephone conversations with her are confusing and disruptive, providing unreliable information. One of the important questions requiring immediate attention is whether Nancy is safe in her isolated home environment. A second is whether she is aware of her declining cognitive and behavioral functioning. For me, hearing of a change in sleep cycle increases my concern of possible wandering. If there is wandering then one must again consider safety.

• There is the possibility that Nancy may not have Alzheimer's disease. Without the children knowing her medical history for a long period of time, they would have to consider other reasons for her decline. Medical records would be necessary to determine preexisting conditions that could account for what the children consider big changes in their mother. In actuality, her behavioral and cognitive decline may be already clearly noted. If Nancy has not recently visited with a medical doctor, a full medical workup in called for. The possibilities of alcohol-related cognitive decline, depression from grief, or improper medication usage are a few possible reasons for her decline other than Alzheimer's disease.

• Having a "separated" family going through the dementia process is a very challenging process. When there is a history of poor communication, residual anger, hurt, and sadness regarding earlier life with a now demented parent, separating current necessary action from past emotional intensity is daunting! Each child is forced to reevaluate his or her level of care and participation with their mother. If there is a *normal* aging process, Nancy could be part of the decision-making, providing clear input as to the type of care she wants and where she would like to live, and completing necessary legal and financial commitments. With dementia, her participation is limited at best. With three children, each has their "back-pack" of burdens from earlier in their lives to drag into the fray. Each child's participation as a caregiver to Nancy will be partially based on the ability to balance the earlier life relationship, which was stormy and lacked the emotional support that Nancy will require as the disease progresses.

• The children now face their changed relationship with each other. How will they manage decision-making responsibilities: from afar, or close? Milt has taken the point position at present. Is he expected to continue in that role? Understanding their relationships earlier in life gives us clues to how they will operate under this duress. Also consider that they have not kept close contact with each other as adults. How will their communication patterns emerge? There is no mention at present about her financial status and who wants to have POA (power of attorney), although each child has thoughts on the matter.

• In this situation, infrequent telephone contact is the norm, not only between each child and the parent, but among the children themselves. Since Robin has been seemingly calling all three children at random, they are all equally apprised regarding her disturbing behaviors. This starts out as a long-distance intervention until it is determined that one of the children must have direct contact with the mother. Choosing Milt is a double-edged sword in this case. On the positive side, Milt is the least confronting based on family history, has had some time to evaluate the situation, and seems to have some relationship with one of his sisters. On the other hand, he could be the most easily swayed and may have to deal with the potential wrath of his older sister. nancy's children have considered her previous relationship with them dysfunctional: they saw her as not available, offering poor emotional support, and passively supporting Dad's drinking.

• Milt's tolerance will be challenged dramatically, and his stress level will rise, as he must wear a number of hats in this situation: assessing the present safety level of their mom, reporting to his sisters about her status, setting up and following through with necessary professional appointments, catching up with any neglected concerns in Mom's life (for how long we are not sure), taking the lead into the next phase of treatment and decision-making (and working with Nancy on that), putting his life on hold to accommodate for his time without knowing the time span this will actually take.

• Both sisters also have their stresses, including long-distance decision-making, dealing with the idea of giving care to someone for whom they have a mixed bag of feelings, or the impact of reinvesting into their roles as sisters and daughters.

• A final question at this point is to determine if it is best to move quickly and get Nancy situated in a more stable location. If her thinking abilities continue to decline, new environments with new faces may increase her level of confusion and anxiety at a faster rate. The first appointments with professionals concerning Nancy's recent changes have begun, and it is imperative that if she is relocated, there is immediate involvement with professional and legal care.

In what ways is the above case different from or similar to your family situation?

_____

_____

_____

_____

_____

_____

CASE 6 Early Phase

Caleb: Father with Alzheimer's   Marge: Deceased wife
Martha: Daughter-in-law   Jaden: Grandson

Caleb lives with his son's family. They built an extension to their house for his privacy, and since the loss of Marge, his wife, they thought it would be better to have him close to be with grandchildren. Jaden, his eight-year-old grandson, has spent many afternoons with "Poppie." Sometimes they read, walk around the mall, or go to the park. Caleb has had several medical problems over the years; he is currently treated for major depression and attends outpatient physical therapy following recent surgery due to a left hip fracture. Since his surgery, Caleb and Jaden have been spending less time together. When not in therapy, Caleb spends increased time alone in his part of the house. When asked to participate in family activities, Caleb attends, but it has become quite difficult. The family notices that Caleb has had difficulty remembering appointments and scheduled times to "watch" Jaden when his parents are out of the house. One time, when they were planning to go out to dinner, the family waited fifteen minutes in the car for Caleb when he said he "forgot my watch" on the dresser. Watching football on television with his son and grandson is no longer the pleasure it was. As a matter of fact, Caleb rarely makes it through an hour-long television program without getting up several times, seemingly distracted, or he falls asleep.

Caleb continues to read the newspaper and can discuss the newsworthy events of the day. He does forget names and occasionally uses the wrong word, or will describe words instead of saying the word itself.; "You know, that thing you write with" rather than saying "pen." Jaden and Caleb laugh about those times. Caleb says that he is trying to teach Jaden new words and practice his old ones. Sitting with Jaden when parents are out continues, with parents coming home to Jaden still awake at midnight and the half-gallon of ice cream, bought that afternoon, gone. Caleb and Jaden love to build with Legos and blocks, but recently Caleb seems to lose patience and appears unable to complete the projects with the enclosed diagrams. Putting together the Lego airplane is no longer possible, so it has become an activity they no longer take time with.

Just the other day, Caleb was helping to clean up the dinner dishes. He took a dish with corn in it and asked his daughter-in-law, Martha, where the "whatchamacallit" goes. She was not looking at him and asked what he was referring to. He responded, saying, "You know, this stuff in the dish. We didn't finish it." Jaden began to giggle. Martha, still busy and not turning around, asked him what he was talking about. Caleb was clearly frustrated with his word loss and Jaden's giggling. Loudly, he said, "The darn leftovers, for heaven's sake. You know what I mean. You don't have to make a deal over this!" Martha turned around, stunned by his loud angry voice; Jaden, looking frightened, moved closer to his mom.

Changes noted in the person with dementia and the family:

In Caleb:
- Caleb remains functionally independent
- Some noted difficulty with role boundaries
- Spending less time with grandson

- Poor retention for keeping appointments and planned caring for grandchild
- Increase in agitation and growing intolerance
- Minor word loss
- Growing difficulty with sequential tasks
- Increased emotional unpredictability
- Growing apathy and lethargy
- Decreased judgment and insight

Effects and Interventions

Effects on the family:

- Caleb's level of participation in family activities has diminished, and this might have several effects. If the periods of his activity continue to diminish, the family could look to alter their schedule to accommodate his lethargy and apathy. This strategy could work and strongly depends on how they approach the matter. If Caleb believes that the family does not consider him able to provide support for Jaden, he will further withdraw and increase his self-doubt. Caleb will tolerate subtle changes as long as he feels needed and important, while the family feels safe with his continued involvement. This will also help to maintain the very important relationship between Caleb and Jaden.

- Signs of Caleb's diminished judgment will affect the decisions parents will make regarding Caleb having time alone with Jaden (driving, responsibility for certain chores, safety issues). It is difficult to determine whether Caleb recognizes his diminished judgment from what was presented in the case. If he does not, accommodations for change, as stated above, must be slow and subtle. There is no substitute for safety, yet there are ways to decrease time periods in which Caleb has complete responsibility for Jaden. If necessary, it may be time to have a medical or behavioral health specialist intervene and give direction for safety concerns.

• As the level of intolerance and agitation rises in Caleb, so may the response style of his son and daughter-in-law. This will fuel the potential of much unspoken resentment, confusion, and withdrawal from Caleb. It will also affect the harmony in the family; more specifically, Jaden may pull away from Caleb or feel forced to "pick sides." Considering that all the family members live in close quarters, daily interaction is unavoidable. Attempting to deny the angst and frustration, which can pile up every day, would be useless. Caleb may be in the early phase of dementia, and it is best now to establish criteria for keeping an effective household.

• It is easy for frustration to increase when someone appears to not be paying attention, or seems easily distracted so that directions or information must be repeated several times daily or over several days. This is common and one of the primary symptoms of early phase Alzheimer's dementia. There are several ways to approach this matter, and any or all suggestions can be used simultaneously. As stated earlier in the book, retention of new information is the first to leave memory. *People with dementia ask repeated question. They do so because they can forget what they just heard, not to upset or cause problems with others.* It can be an entire phrase or a few words. Their forgetting depends on how tired they are, distractions in the environment, who may be talking to them, what the message is or in how complicated a manner it is presented.

When I want someone to hear my message clearly, I make sure they are listening by establishing eye contact, having minimal distractions, and keeping my message clear and succinct. Use these strategies. The more direct, short, and clear your message, the better chance of reception and retention. At this phase, new information should be presented several times with written notes or posted reminders. For example, with Caleb, I might put up reminders for appointments somewhere in his apartment so it becomes routine for him to check that area. Daily schedules with specific times attached on a white board work well and can be changed daily.

• With word loss and/or misuse, there is a tendency to finish the thought or phrase for the person, where actually, more patience is required. As with completing tasks, people with Alzheimer's dementia begin to require additional time to process incoming information, comprehend the information, and finally decide how to respond. This is a complex cognitive procedure involving a number of steps that most of us do instantaneously. Each segment of the process requires different skills. At this point in the disease, most people will be able to complete the cognitive tasks before them. *Let them go at their own pace.* Slightly struggling with understanding and reporting information may be challenging to an individual, but challenge is what is needed now. This may be tricky. If a person absolutely cannot remember a name or what the proper word is and begins to get frustrated or angry, then assist by cueing their memory. It is a delicate balance when one knows the person is forgetting and is, as a result, frightened.

• Pressuring loved ones with Alzheimer's to attend family outings or a social situation when they want to be detached produces a dilemma for them. On one hand they may feel they are not able to keep up with the other members of the family, and, on the other hand, they really want that sense of safety being around their family members. This is an unsolvable bind! As stated in the earlier comments, finding that balance in the family is crucial, especially if the family lives together or sees each other daily. Outings can be for less time, be planned closer to home, and involve fewer people, if necessary. By design, some family outings may be for younger family members and the elders may not attend. The busy, highly stimulating museum, park, or baseball games may not have the grab for the Alzheimer's person, who would appreciate a more intimate setting with fewer people and less action.

• Jaden is eight years old and, at first, will not understand the cognitive miscues as a problem. He will laugh at Poppie, and hopefully Poppie will laugh with him. As time goes on, Jaden will become frightened at the frequency of times Poppie says something "silly" or his mood suddenly shifts because he forgot the name of an item. It is imperative to talk directly to the child by **STATING THE OBVIOUS.** Make sure the child knows that **THIS IS NOT THEIR FAULT.** To younger children, I might say, *"Poppie gets tired easier and it is harder for him to have as much fun when there are a lot of people and noise around. When he gets tired, he sometimes forgets words or what he was saying. He still loves you dearly. If you have any questions or feel worried, let Dad or me know."* There is no way around this change and growing reality. Poppie is changing, and his relationship with *EVERYONE* will change. This is what the disease does to families. In the moderate and advanced phases of Alzheimer's, the effect on children and teens becomes more intense and difficult. I will discuss those changes more in the chapters dedicated to moderate and advanced phase cases. There are a number of children's books and pamphlets for parents that may be obtained through local chapters, or the national chapter, of the Alzheimer's Association.

• In this case, there was mention that Caleb suffers from major depression. In the elderly, depression may present with similar symptoms found in mild cognitive impairment or Alzheimer's disease. Depression could mask dementia symptoms or the dementia symptoms could be more pronounced due to depression. Isolation, lethargy, and possibly some of the cognitive concerns expressed in the case may be due to significant depression, or the combination of depression and Alzheimer's disease. For example, a person with early dementia may not want to participate in family activities because they suffer from depression or, they get easily confused with high environmental stimulation. Consult a mental health specialist who could assist in clarifying the implications for continuing treatment.

In what ways is the above case different from or similar to your family situation?

_____

_____

_____

_____

_____

_____

CASE 7 Early Phase

Donnell: Father with Alzheimer's disease
Beau: Son

Donnell is a retired 72-year-old man living by himself in a retirement community, which he and his wife moved to six years ago. Two years ago his wife died of breast cancer. Donnell's usual day consists of eating breakfast by himself and either going to the community center to play cards or going to the fitness center. He goes home for lunch or dines with friends and their wives at the clubhouse. After the meal, he goes back to his condo and relaxes with the newspaper, watches some television, or naps. Following dinner, he takes a walk or attends social event and follows this with a good night's sleep. He has no sleep problems. He takes medications for high blood pressure and cholesterol and several over-the-counter supplemental vitamins. He has a son and family within ten miles with whom he is very close: he has regular visits with the grandchildren, another son two days' travel away, and a daughter currently living with her family in England.

Over the course of the past month, Donnell has not been attending to his daily routine. Friends have noticed that he is not joining them regularly at the fitness center nor the clubhouse, and when he does, his clothes are disheveled and wrinkled. Donnell appears tired and, at times, unshaven. When asked why he is not showing up, he offers vague responses. Conversations with Donnell have become shorter, without much detail, and when asked about his family, he replies to one friend "they are good" and on another occasion, to the same person, "I have not heard from any of my family in months." Donnell does not attend evening social events any more, and while he still goes for walks, it has been reported that he is out at one or two in the morning walking around the community. Donnell had been an avid bridge player but recently stopped playing, stating that he tires quickly. Other players reported that he takes longer to play his cards and has difficulty following the game.

These changes were discovered by his family when his son, Beau, came to visit. He arrived mid-morning expecting to find his dad at the fitness center. When he could not find him, he asked a close friend where he was and heard the above details. His son went to his dad's condo and found him sitting in a recliner chair with the television and radio on. He was wearing gym shorts and no shirt. When Beau asked his dad what was going on, Donnell immediately jumped up and said he was going to the fitness center. He did not ask any questions about Beau being at his condo.

Beau learned firsthand about the changes that were taking place. He observed the poor hygiene and nutrition and the general lack of cleanliness in the condo, and he discovered that his dad was not keeping up with his financial obligations (paying monthly bills). Beau, along with his wife, decided that they would spend more time at the condo, hire a person to clean and help prepare meals, and take over the management of his dad's resources and financial obligations. Beau met with high resistance to his taking over financial duties and backed away when Donnell stated, "I do not want anyone to spend or take my money!" There were steps to be taken by the family, and it was clear that Donnell would be resistant.

Changes noted in the person with dementia and the family:

In Donnell:
- Recent change: not following through with established routine
- Personal hygiene changes; clothes disheveled and unclean
- Problems keeping track of time
- Less verbal communication
- Not attending evening social events
- Has been seen walking at all hours of the night by himself
- Slower processing and difficulty with 'step' activities (e.g., bridge)
- Not keeping up with monthly financial responsibilities
- Resistance to Beau's assistance with financial issues—denial of problems and possible paranoia

In Beau:
1. Decides to spend more time at the condo with his dad
2. Wants to hire someone to come into the condo for housekeeping purposes
3. Attempts to take control of his dad's finances and backs down when he complains

Effects and Interventions

• Donnell has decided to stop playing cards and in general has begun to withdraw from his social environment. There could be several reasons for his changes. In the early phase of the disease, the person with Alzheimer's begins to have difficulty judging situations and takes increased time to filter verbal messages from social interplay. Their ability to focus and not be distracted is tested in social situations and with games of any sort; there is a norm for pace and rules. Learning new information will test a person with cognitive impairment, with increased retention problems and the potential for misinterpretations. Friends may not understand Donnell's situation and add fuel to the fire with jokes and comments. Another possible interpretation of Donnell's withdrawal from social events is the increasing difficulty with games and projects that require *steps* or *sequencing*. Bridge requires multiple thoughts at the same time, projecting future moves based on your cards and on others' play, and clear retention of cards played.

• Personal hygiene concerns are arising, with Donnell's disheveled appearance at the fitness center and his son finding him partially clothed at his condo. Is this due to general apathy, depression, or having difficulty with task completion? Additionally, Donnell is beginning to use tools he has for minor repairs inappropriately, and forgets their proper use. Nutrition is one aspect of hygiene. Whether a person forgets to eat, has difficulty preparing meals, or becomes apathetic to the preparation, there is a considerable danger of serious health problems arising that could mask the underlying dementia.

• Another concern regards Donnell's late night walks. This is new behavior, but not unusual as this disease progresses; it is not uncommon to have a person's internal clock vary, changing hours in their sleep/wake cycle. When a person is living alone, it is a common symptom that is overlooked.

In general, as one ages, less sleep time is required, and family members may minimize or ignore the parent's four-hour sleep nights or early rising. Another element concerning the wandering is the safety issue. The person with Alzheimer's may wander out of their neighborhood and get lost, misinterpreting signs or locations.

• One would have to question Donnell's orientation at times. Having the television and radio on at the same time and his contradictory responses when others ask about his family display a lack of clarity and reasoning. Reasoning can also be questioned with his vague communication with his family and the mixed messages he gives to others regarding his state of affairs. Clear orientation is inversely related to confusion. The higher the confusion, the more errors of time, place, and understanding. For the individual suffering from dementia, the higher the activity level, the higher the risk for confusion and the more noticeable the decline if others are paying attention.

• Donnell has led an independent lifestyle for a number of years and is highly resistive to assistance with his financial situation and general well-being. Through lack of contact, Donnell has withdrawn from his family. He is no longer talking to his grandchildren, and his communication with children is becoming less frequent. Depending on the age of the grandchildren, the lack of contact could be powerful, especially if Donnell played a larger role earlier in their life. What would the children be told, and how could they be re-integrated into Donnell's life comfortably? The first steps would be educating the children to the present situation with their grandfather, and reviewing their expectations of the relationship so as to help Donnell adjust to his limitations. This will also help to address the general denial issues that Donnell will be experiencing at this time.

• Beau is *intruding* into Donnell's life. There will be resistance from Donnell to most of what Beau will offer. Again, this is not unusual as Donnell has become very accustomed to his *independent* lifestyle, but because of his denial and minimizing the obvious changes, he does not easily observe his decline. The family has been "out of the loop" when it comes to the changes taking place in Donnell's life. Up to this point Donnell has presented well enough with his family that they would dismiss any "odd" behavior and not be able to notice the pattern that was forming. His resistance could cloud judgment regarding his cognitive slippage. Beau has a difficult task before him. There are necessary changes to be considered that will impact the entire family. Whatever decision is reached, the family will require formidable sacrifices if they are to remain intimately involved. Considering that Donnell is in an early phase of the disease, once he has established a new routine and feels comfortable, he may begin to more rigorously resist family involvement.

• When Beau arrived at Donnell's condo, he was stirred into action. This meant a new level of involvement, with increased time and energy commitment, for which he and his family were unprepared. Where does Donnell's son start? How does he determine what to focus on? Getting a sense of the totality of the situation may take some time. First, Beau must determine if Donnell is safe. There will be reticence from Donnell to honestly share all that has changed. He might not even be aware of the subtle changes already in progress. Speaking to friends would be helpful, but Beau must careful not to embarrass his father or let his own judgment be swayed by others who are only privy to their intermittent observations. As Donnell is in the early part of the first phase, presenting the concerns in an adult, non-emotional manner would be best. I would approach this with the idea of seeking a medical checkup to obtain a professional opinion as to the degree of cognitive loss *or* other medical or psychological problem that may be influencing Donnell's changes.

• Donnell's changes have been successfully hidden until recently. They have become more prolific; there is an increase in his decline, or he is losing his ability to contain the course of his losses. Friends have noticed that Donnell is no longer participating and socializing daily. If Donnell continues to live in his condo, how will he adjust to less social companionship? One of Donnell's friends shared information with Beau, but do any of them want to become caregivers if Donnell continues to fail? Families must realize the jeopardy they put a loved one in by ignoring the potential dangers of relying on *others* to keep track or monitor their family member. At present, there is no official diagnosis for Donnell's fluctuating status. What if he is diagnosed with Alzheimer's dementia? At what point does a new plan go into effect—housing, care-giving, medical/behavioral health attention?

• We are not clear about Beau's relationship with his siblings. Their communication becomes a major factor in determining Donnell's future. What is their history together? Have they been involved in other life-changing situations together and how have they moved through them? Are there financial or health consideration that must be accounted for? There are a number of other questions that could arise in another family. Carefully consider yours, as family dynamics are fluid and contain trace elements of guilt, shame, grief, and resentments. It is urgent that family members who wish to be part of the care-giving process decide clearly and early about how to manage the current and upcoming affairs. This would be best accomplished with a meeting of all family members at the earliest convenience.

• In this case, the children have had intermittent contact with their grandfather. Depending on the way they spent time, younger grandchildren will giggle over Grandpa's mistakes and forgetfulness. It will be difficult for them to notice the changes from visit to visit, and if they do, they may be less likely to talk about them with parents. Grandfather may stop certain activities, like completing puzzles and playing card games, and may lose attention while they read to him. Younger children who do notice these changes may actually become increasingly verbally protective of Grandpa and do more for him. Teens may begin to lose patience with his cognitive errors, repetitive questions, and inability to follow complex discussions and games. They may tend to correct Grandpa, which may, in turn, cause him to become increasingly agitated or withdraw from family interaction.

In what ways is the above case different from or similar to your family situation?

_____

_____

_____

_____

_____

_____

CREATING AN ACTION PLAN

Now that you have read the cases illustrating the challenges of this phase of Alzheimer's disease, you may fill in the spaces after the following action items. I hope this can serve as a starting point to develop a plan for how you will move through the transitions that the disease brings about.

What concrete plans must be put into motion at this time?

_____

_____

_____

_____

_____

Who will be in charge of implementing the plans?

_____

_____

_____

_____

Do you require an action plan for medical, psychiatric, or legal assistance?

_____

_____

_____

_____

_____

What professionals or organizations will need to be contacted?

_____

_____

_____

_____

_____

Who will be the "Point Person" in charge of coordinating care needs with professionals and handling the unforeseen and acute situations that will arise?

_____

_____

_____

_____

What support networks need to be established to provide care and education for family members?

_____

_____

_____

_____

_____

_____

Chapter 2

Alzheimer's Dementia: Moderate Phase

Believe in miracles

But prepare for alternatives

Anonymous

Segment One:
Overview

In the moderate phase of Alzheimer's disease, the family is fully aware of the cognitive and behavioral changes that have taken place and they have begun the long difficult period of transitions that will set the stage for the remainder of the affected person's life. The family adjustments may affect all facets of their lives. There could be changes in residence for the person with Alzheimer's and many episodes of potentially unpleasant interaction with family members. In general terms, passing through the moderate phase of the disease, the affected person recognizes there are deficiencies in his or her functioning. The person with Alzheimer's can become easily confused and frustrated, which leads to increasing impulsiveness and a less inhibited response style. This phase of the disease sees the largest change in functional independent cognition and behavior. Therefore, the family stress increases, with roles and relations altered to accommodate the disease. The dramatic alteration in independent functioning and reliance on family poses an extraordinary altering of how the family system is defined. **At some point during this phase, families with a loved one who has Alzheimer's should consider a more secure level of care than the home environment, for the safety and health of the affected loved one and that of the care-giving family.** Therefore, building *family consensus* in the decision-making process is essential to providing the best possible care, the greatest degree of family involvement, and a key way to reduce stress and second-guessing in the future. Families build upon their confidence and knowledge through open discussions, disagreements, and the development of trust in one other.

Making critical independent decisions for our own betterment is a highly prized self-identifying function that we all cherish; it is something that helps to define OUR life as separate from others. Choosing, for instance, the best health care policy uses the ability to process (take in the information clearly and completely), to judge which information is best suited for our needs, and to understand the implications of our decision about which policy we choose (how will our decision affect our life now and in the future: health concerns, financial limitations, assistance needed for care). During this moderate phase of dementia, those abilities noticeably diminish. As understanding and providing clear messages becomes more difficult, confusion, along with feeling overloaded with details, fosters frustration with the process and the deliverer of the information, which increases the level of agitation in the communications.

During this phase, the person with Alzheimer's loses the ability to think abstractly, so information is processed concretely, using cognitive skills based on behavioral signs and observations ("What I observe is what I understand," which can constitute a poor application of one situation to another). Here is an example:

Bonnie is discussing with her psychologist her husband's strong desire to go to the central library at the state university. Chris is in the moderate phase of Alzheimer's dementia. Each time she comes to visit at the assisted living facility, he says, "I want to go to the state library." He was an avid reader and wants to continue his "reading" (he no longer reads more than a few sentences at a time and has poor retention of new material). Chris is unsteady on his feet and requires a wheelchair outside of his room at the local assisted living facility. The distance from where you would park your car to the entrance of the library is approximately 1/8 mile. Bonnie decides that she will take Chris to the local library, which is a shorter "wheeling" distance, to judge whether or not she has the ability to push him a longer distance in his wheelchair. She reasons that if she has no problem with that shorter distance, the longer distance would be okay. When I ask her what she would do if she had difficulty at the local library, she stated that she would tell Chris that she could not wheel him the 1/8 mile two ways and would not take him to the state library.

Bonnie is using sound judgment....for herself! Her decision to take or not take Chris to the state university library is solely based on her ability to wheel Chris the 1/8 mile distance two ways. In her thinking ,Chris will understand that since she cannot wheel him the shorter distance at the local library, she would not be able to wheel him at the state library. This kind of reasoning supposes that her husband understands the implications of the current situation and can *apply* that information to a future event. It will not happen!

Segment Two:
Family Considerations

This is the time to look at partial or full-time in-home care, *OR* look into a more restricted quieter environment for the person with Alzheimer's. With the dramatic changes occurring during this phase of the disease, it is imperative for the family to *re-create itself* in order to function at a level of safety. If the affected loved one is currently living with family, it is now imperative to ask whether it is safe for the affected person to remain in the home or to consider placement into a more structured environment such as a group home, assisted living facility, or skilled nursing facility with or without a special dementia unit. Criteria to consider regarding this possible life-changing family decision include:

- **Cognition:** Is the person with dementia capable of making personal decisions that reflect safety, insight, judgment, reasoning, and planning? Social and personal decisions regarding safety, hygiene, finances, medication, mobility, and nutrition are compromised by diminished cognitive status. The higher the level of confusion, the higher the potential for error, poor communication, and stress among the family members. Grandchildren and adult children can lose perspective on how to communicate effectively with their loved one. In the latter part of this phase, the affected loved one loses the ability to use logic as a means to find solutions, while the family tends to continue using logic to explain events. Pattern following, abstract thinking, and sequencing abilities disappear and are replaced with more concrete one-step thinking processes. Also possibly emerging at this time are delusions, or distortions, of reality. Misperceptions of the environment caused by decreasing cognitive abilities, poorly interpreted cues, or increased fear and agitation will occur. The delusions are frightening for the entire family, and the potential for confusing or aggressive response from the family member with Alzheimer's increases. Grandchildren and teens are most vulnerable to the physical reactions of their grandparent. Reminiscence activities can help the person with Alzheimer's with lowering distortion of memories, with feeling safer in the new environment, and with cueing for daily routine. Photos, other visual reminders, and music are often used to help people with dementia.

- **Continence Status (Loss of ability to control elimination of urine or feces):** With incontinence come embarrassment, denial, secrecy, covering up, and resentment. The potential for role confusion and role switching increases. Personal hygiene concerns increase for all of the family in common areas. Younger children will be confused and shy away from grandparents, while teens may react with disgust, resent the presence of the grandparent, and not want any peers in the home. If it is time for the grandparent to wear protective undergarments, there could be resistance and anger, which further fuels the problem.

- **Fall Risk:** Three-generation family homes are active and cluttered. Toys, clothes, newspapers, and other objects may be left around the home with minimal thought of how an older person could be at risk. Additionally, our pace of moving about the home is quicker and we generally do not *watch our edges* as closely as folks who are more fragile and cautious. It is frightening to watch an older person fall; reaction and response are slower in seniors, and their bones are brittle. If we add some confusion, the potential for injury increases. Homes that are designed for the older generation to live with adult children and grandchildren generally have separate areas for private living space and can design space with safety in mind. Reminding younger children about the fall and health risks of their grandparents will also aid in preventing incidents.

- **Functional Capacity:** Functional capacity relates to how well a person can perform expected activities independently, and possibly in tandem with others, to make daily living manageable. As a person becomes less functional and has increased difficulty caring for daily living needs, there is added strain on others in the household to assist or take over additional responsibilities. The impending stress will affect each family member differently and may increase tension in relationships. Some tasks may continue to be performed by the affected loved one but require monitoring or after-the-fact checks, which will take up more of the time and patience of other family members. Reducing the number of tasks that the affected loved one is responsible for could help for a period of time but, in combination with other criteria, may not be practical for long.

- **Mood:** As discussed with cases in Chapter 1 and in more detail in Chapter 4, it is apparent that people with Alzheimer's disease begin to have increased mood changes as their confusion and general debility increase. Mood changes can be stimulated by environmental triggers, by frustration at the increasing inability to perform or think clearly, by misinterpretation of cues, or by the disease process itself. As the Alzheimer's progresses, mood changes can occur rapidly, without warning, and frighten children who are unprepared and do not understand the nature of the changes in their grandparent. Let's suppose that Grandpa, who lives with his son and family and has been diagnosed with early or moderate phase Alzheimer's, goes with his daughter-in-law to pick the children up after school. The children are happy to see Grandpa and are both talking at once, telling him about what they brought to school for show and tell. Grandpa is overwhelmed with the influx of stimulation from the children. He is trying to listen and keep focus on the road at the same time. His ability to manage the situation drops and there is no escape. Without any warning, he suddenly turns to the children and yells at them to *"shut the heck up."* There is silence in the car. Handling a situation like that is difficult for all the participants. What effect will that have on the relationship between Grandpa and the children? Is this the first time the explosive anger has been revealed? How should the daughter-in-law handle the event?

- **Nutrition:** One of the difficult transitions families make in living with a person who has Alzheimer's disease is re-learning how to communicate with simple words and slow presentation. For a person with Alzheimer's disease, completing tasks that require multiple steps becomes a problematic endeavor and potentially dangerous. This is very apparent with cooking and general intake of food and liquids. Preparing meals becomes a burden, with missed ingredients and danger involving the use of gadgetry, ovens, stoves, etc. Making meals simpler means less nutrition, eating at varying hours, and changes in taste likes and dislikes. Commonly, there are changes in the internal clock of the person with dementia. If he or she is awake during the night and getting something to eat, established *family time* meals will become more difficult. A person with Alzheimer's disease may find eating at night alone is less confusing and more relaxing, without the high energy of the grandchildren or other environmental stimulation during the meal.

- **Social Support:** Numerous times I have heard family members state, "She needs her family. We can provide the safety and support she needs. We keep her active, get her to appointments, make sure someone is home at all times to care for her, and we know she will be happier here than in a nursing home." This may be true, but at what cost to the family members who must extend themselves and their days to accommodate the appointments and needs of the their loved one? At this point in the disease process, the family member with Alzheimer's dependency needs increase, which promotes an emergence of *tailgat-*

ing or *shadowing* the other family members. Fear and insecurity grow, and the desire to be closer to known persons further accentuates the strain on the caregivers and family members. Many studies have shown that one important factor in maintaining health as a person ages is the social network that has been established outside of the home. Peers who are of similar age and background tend to motivate and generate continuing activity. At this point in the disease process, people with Alzheimer's disease can find appropriate community day resources and continue to maintain personal relationships with closer friends aware of the affected person's *potholes and limits*. Having the family take sole responsibility for all entertainment, safety, and routines of their loved one is a dangerous, and often times short, road to travel.

- **Vision/Hearing:** This is another factor involved in the safety realm. Obviously, the risk of falling and other dangers become a higher potential when a person has visual or hearing complications. In a home where grandparents spend time reading to or with grandchildren, visual deficits begin to be a determent for time together. More and brighter lights need to be on; reading newspapers and magazines become problematic, and if time reading drops, how will the person with dementia pass the time? Preparing food, hygiene, dressing, and a number of other daily routine tasks become a hardship which can affect mood and the relationships in the home. Poor hearing can have the same effect. The television must be uncomfortably loud to others. Often, family members must repeat themselves to be heard and understood, so that spending time in social situations becomes stressed. A combination of cognitive decline and visual/hearing impairment may create a triad of danger, stress, and anger that tests the ability of families to remain cohesive.

- **Co-existing Medical Concerns:** It is uncommon that a person will pass solely due to the effects of Alzheimer's disease alone. In most situations, there are co-existing medical problems that diminish the strength and general health of the person with dementia. I have worked with families where heart disease, cancer, pneumonia, or other debilitating diseases have been the exacerbating reason for a person's passing. Having to use oxygen machines, walkers, or other medical apparatus that must be present in the home or when the person leaves the home can create a myriad of problems for caregivers and grandchildren. Along with the other medical conditions comes the regimen of medicine allocation, and then the issue of safety for the younger children with these medications in the home. Additionally, there will be an increase in appointments and consultations with medical professionals outside the home. The possibilities of having emergency service personnel enter your home due to a fall or chest pain can be a harrowing experience for all. Seeing Grandpa rolled out by EMS responders could be a traumatic experience for any family members. Routine consultation with professionals is important for maintaining the growing health needs of your loved one with dementia as the ability to schedule, attend, understand, and follow recommendations decreases. Families may see an increase in bruising, falls and other acute conditions as the affected loved one loses the ability to effectively communicate needs. The clear expression of needs decreases with the increase in infection, pain, lowered tolerance, agitation, and delusions about what may be wrong. Hospitalizations for medical concerns and/or use of anesthesia could exacerbate cognitive difficulties and the person with Alzheimer's may not regain the former level of functioning.

- **Spirituality:** Most people who come from a family system where a particular religious or spiritual preference was practiced generally ignore the spiritual hardship early in the disease. As the disease begins to dominate the affected person's personality and behavior, maintaining a strong belief system is severely challenged. *"Why is this happening to him?"; "How could G-d allow for someone to go through this torture?" "What did she ever do to deserve this?"; "He would never hurt anyone!"* are some of the phrases I have heard in my years in practice. There are so many unanswerable questions, there does not seem to be any logical reason for the suffering a person goes through. As the disease progresses, praying, meditation or attending any form of spiritual activity may offer solace on a personal basis. Personal faith IS put to the test!

These factors require an ongoing assessment of the feasibility of having your affected family member remain in the family home; ideally, they will prompt the family to identify and plan toward the impending rough spots, anticipate the needs of all family members, maintain active family involvement, minimize secrets, and use outside resources for optimizing support. Each family system is different; each can afford varying financial assistance and provide varying time and energy to support their loved one.

Segment Three:
Changes in Cognition

Aphasia: The ability of the affected loved one to express *and* receive information clearly and with understanding greatly diminishes over this period. There is increased word loss and substitution with tendencies to become repetitive and focused in verbal communications. Retention of new information is greatly diminished, processing slowed, and judgment hampered. As a result, people with Alzheimer's can become *fixated* on certain issues. They also find it difficult to let go of information they may partially understand, and they have trouble finding the words to talk about what is on their mind.

Apraxia: It is sometimes difficult to determine whether the person with Alzheimer's has trouble dressing because of memory problems and lacks the ability to grasp the logical sequence of the task, or because of loss of previously possessed ability to perform skilled and purposeful motor acts. Later in the disease process, this is shown through the loss of ability to use an eating utensil or a telephone.

Agnosia: As the disease progresses, visual information becomes distorted in the brain. The ability to recognize familiar faces slowly decreases and is why the affected family member may not readily identify, without cueing, family members who have not been with the person with Alzheimer's for several months. Visual-spatial cues in the environment are missed or misinterpreted, and your loved one may require additional cuing for daily routine or recognition of regular visitors and once-familiar objects. Abstract reasoning construction and spatial orientation is vastly diminished late in this phase. Asking a person in this phase to explain the meaning of the phrase "a bird in the hand is worth two in the bush" would produce highly concrete responses about having a bird in their hand without the understanding of the more abstract interpretations.

Memory: Loss of recent and short-term memory is impaired, with growing distortion of time and logic, proper order of events, the confusion of combining events of one memory with another and faulty sequencing of information. Therefore, information presented by the person with Alzheimer's becomes unreliable, and secondary sources are needed for confirmation.

Calculation: Basic math skills are eroding. The person with Alzheimer's can no longer balance a checkbook or be safe to go shopping alone. The ability to sequence numbers necessary for adding and subtracting is compromised, especially when multiple items and sets of numbers are involved. Pressure, confusion, and embarrassment further exacerbate such situations.

An important factor that further compromises the affected person's cognitive abilities is the continuing motor system changes. The increase in pacing and restlessness, in combination with cognitive slippage, in the confined spaces of the home may hinder time playing or sitting with grandchildren and will raise the general tension level in the family.

Segment Four:
Accommodations for Care

1. **Safety:** As stated earlier, when a person suffers from mild cognitive impairment or mild dementia, there are beginning concerns about the tendency of the person with Alzheimer's to minimize, deny, or substitute for cognitive decline or behavioral gaffes. Since the family member with Alzheimer's remains quite functional in everyday life, others in the family may ignore or devalue the importance of the changes taking place. During the moderate phase, Alzheimer's affords these "luxuries" no more. There is clear debilitation with recognizing safety concerns and inability to function independently. It is during this phase that important decisions need to be made in areas of finances, living arrangements, medical and psychiatric directives, family commitments, family responsibilities, and safety precautions. Safety also includes family member protection, in the face of perceived obligation to the person with Alzheimer's that may conflict with responsibility to the larger family unit. If obligation to the affected family member reflects a commitment from a prior time in life, guilt and resentment become unwelcome partners in the decision-making process. **"Too often people put expectations solely on themselves regarding care for others based on "should, ought to, and supposed to."** Each family faces personal struggles not to be judged

by this author or any other observer. Safety reflects the behavior and decision-making of the affected loved one in tandem with decisions made by others providing that person's care. Misjudging whether a person can drive, be left alone with young children, or manage finances or medical decisions may permanently impact a person or a family system to cause emotional harm or over reactions in the future.

2. **Flow of communication:** The "common" or "little" mistakes observed in the early phase are more frequent and more serious. Simple gestures and words may not be understood clearly, which could involve increasingly serious consequences. Tasks that require several steps may remain incomplete or result in errors. The person with Alzheimer's is no longer able to balance the checkbook, bake the cake, or make the plane reservations. Another area of communication that begins to suffer is planning and keeping appointments. As the person with Alzheimer's moves through this phase, there is an increase in distortion of time-sense and poor organization of thoughts and planning for events. Misinterpretation of messages can cause impulsive behavioral responses and frequent mood changes. The person with Alzheimer's continues to have social contacts, although these present with increased problems. With declining ability to process incoming information with accuracy and clarity, navigating the meaning of social discussions becomes confusing, intimidating, and frustrating. For example, you are at a dinner with neighbors and people are talking and laughing about how the wives help their husbands with matching clothes, and the way the

husbands hang on to old jeans and shirts with holes. Each wife or husband has a story to tell, and as you tell your story; your husband (who has been diagnosed with dementia and shows signs common during this phase) begins to get visually uncomfortable and agitated, and walks away. Later, at home, he verbally condemns your *revealing personal information about your marriage to others and making him look like a fool to strangers.* His perception of the situation is distorted and confused, and with limited understanding of context in a situation, he is becoming more fearful and protective.

As discussed in Chapter 2, reminiscence activities, like looking at old photos of friends and family members, playing earlier life music and other *reminders* of the former life of the person with dementia helps them to retain a sense of who they are. Anchoring activities, such as practicing addition, playing computer games or using certain tools, are used to help the person with dementia continue at their present skill levels. These techniques are important strategies to help keep communication and skill level at peak performance.

3. **Attention to medical, legal, and social concerns:** As noted in the early phase overview, it is imperative to **plan ahead.** As this is the phase of significant social decline, the attention to medical and legal issues move to the fore. As the *cognitive walls* begin to close around the person with Alzheimer's, it is important to consider the legal and medical implications of life to come. As with all people in a demented person's life, familiarity becomes a central factor during this phase. Forgetting

names turns into forgetting people, specific relationship ties turn into vague memories without specific content, and ongoing medical issues are forgotten, distorted, or ignored. Establishing a sound medical team (family physician, specialists, therapists), with whom the affected person has regular appointments covering specific topics of health and an easy routine for visits, should begin as early as possible. This includes a family physician with knowledge of the affected loved one's (and spouse's) general health and history (and spouse), and specialists who can provide information regarding the physical and mental health changes the family can expect to encounter as the disease progresses. Through this phase, *the decision-maker* becomes the evil person limiting the affected loved one in all facets of life. The professional's decisions begin to carry increased weight, and the person with Alzheimer's will frequently state, "The doctor said I could...," hearing a part of the message or taking a piece out of context. Having a professional astute and knowledgeable about the patterns of dementia is helpful and possibly staves off much emotional turmoil for the caregivers. Having sound legal documents (advanced directives) in place that clarify directions of care, allocations of financial decisions, and who is responsible for those decisions with a power of attorney (POA), needs to be done well in advance of the confusion and paranoia that appears in this phase (these issues will be discussed in greater detail in the moderate-phase cases).

4. **Development of a long-range action plan:** By this time it is imperative that plans are already complete, or in

the process of completion. The long-range action plan described in the overview section of the early phase chapter is now considered the short-range action plan. Due to the immediacy of some situations and the lack of predictability regarding how this disease will progress, once you start playing catch-up with planning, your stress level will multiply rapidly. If family members from afar become involved during this phase, it means more complicated decision-making, with more paperwork, explanation, arrangements, and cost. The main facets of a plan to consider include: care-giving roles, decision-making responsibilities (who makes which decisions when), living arrangements (current and future), when to involve professionals and for what considerations (driving or other restrictions), and financial and legal rules and roles. There are surely other important considerations that will vary with situation and family.

5. **The challenge of change:** There is nothing subtle about the behavioral and personality changes that occur with the person suffering from Alzheimer's during this phase. They are daily and obvious. Challenges are more stressful, create a more emotional setting for all involved with the disease, and generally demand increased attention on a daily basis. These transformations in the affected loved one have "red alert" warning signals flashing for the family, if they are not prepared! The number one concern has to be any children who are involved with their grandparent suffering from Alzheimer's. As previously stated, during the earlier phase, children and teens notice some of the subtle ways their grandparent responds, or not, to given sit-

uations. They are often ready to forgive or overlook the "forgetting" or "mistakes" and will often assist the family in creating a sense of *normalcy*. Now, there is no longer anything subtle about the forgetting, sudden mood switches, apathy, or distancing that the grandparent demonstrates. It is more unsettling for younger children as they do not understand the "flip-flops" of the grandparent and are frightened, maybe feeling some ownership or withdrawing from a significant person. As we will see, children, in their young child way, may mirror some of what they notice in their grandparent. Older children and teens may respond with less time around the grandparent, anger, or exhibiting demanding behaviors of their own from their parents.

The alterations occurring in the family during this phase set the tone for the advanced phase involvement. Family members and friends may come or go. New friends appear and old friends move on. How the family shifts and remains flexible is a key to successful care in the future. I have worked with many families in which the spouse or significant other to the loved one with Alzheimer's has had high expectations from family members as the stress level and commitment level rises, only to feel alone and abandoned in a crisis. I remind people regularly to **watch your edges—in** other words, **pay attention to your limits and abilities, and know when to ask for or demand assistance. Stay within the scope of your health!**

6. **Grief:** When a loved one is diagnosed with Alzheimer's disease, our grieving process begins. The changes that

occur with the individual remind us daily that the person we knew is no longer available, and we must now face an ever-changing person with remnants of his or her former self. It is during this phase that the most remarkable alterations in personality occur. This is not like the earlier phase, where "intrusions into the personality" appear as an interruption of normalcy. **Now, change is the *normal*!** Nor is it like the advanced phase, when people with Alzheimer's are rooted in the disease, with a pronounced loss of their identity and mere, if any, glimpses of their earlier life and being. It is during this time that we observe helplessly the degradation of self, the loss of self-pride, initiative, and evidence of the person we knew! We are saying goodbye to the mother, father, grandpa, or grandma that we knew and loved. We are attempting to accept the certain.

7. **Guilt:** My belief is that guilt harbors anger and has a *capital S "Should" or" Should have"* attached to whatever the situation is about. Up front it is important to admit that **you are powerless to do anything about the onset and outcome of Alzheimer's disease**. I have worked with numerous families that do hold guilt about their history with the disease, or how they were slow to act when signs were evident. The strength of our resistance to acknowledge change, especially if it is negative and it concerns the safety or health of loved ones, can be profound. As previously noted, denying and minimizing are methods we use to protect ourselves from pain and change. I worked with a woman whose earlier life with her mother was traumatic. Her biological dad was not involved, and her mother went through a number of marriages and relationships with boyfriends. This had

negative effects on building trust and safety between my patient and her mother. Now, with her mother in her late 80s, the daughter is faced with a choice either to care for her mother with dementia and provide the kind of support that she did not receive as a child, or to turn her back on the situation and live a non-involved life. This adult child still suffers her loss yet feels strong guilt about not providing for her mother's needs. What is she to do? There is a part of her that would like to walk away and let her non-providing mother fend for herself in the "system," but another part feels that at some time in the future she will be left with strong guilt for not helping her. Their past is a powerful piece in this yet to be completed puzzle!

In the moderate phase of the disease, we are most likely to observe that some close friends have a high level of denial and minimizing of symptoms. This can produce anger or resentment and distancing from the person with Alzheimer's. This is inevitable and will occur at all phases, but it is most noticeable during this time. Family decisions may make it more difficult for friends to spend time with the person with Alzheimer's. The affected loved one may move closer to or move in with family or to a more restricted living arrangement. The combination of increasingly restricted activity level and social calendar coupled with mentation changes may result in reduced time with friends. Awareness of the changes, the loss of friendships can increase depression, fear, and anxiety in the person with Alzheimer's.

We begin to forget the person as they were and may want to forget the person as they are.

SUPPORTING CASES

The following cases present PATTERNS of signs and symptoms that are common to families with similar circumstances at this phase of the disease. Not all changes in the person with Alzheimer's can be fully attributed to the advancement of dementia. Previously existing problems caused by co-existing disease processes, environmental or social factors, or medicine reactions may cause or exacerbate the dementia symptoms.

I am presenting these cases from my practice (names and details have been changed) to help give you a sense of the scope of how the disease presents itself, and the effects it can have on family systems. Your family situation will differ from the presented cases in various ways. **At the end of each case** *presentation and discussion, you'll find space where you can consider how your family situation is like or not like that case.*

As you read the cases, consider the following action items, as a starting point to develop a plan for how you will move through the transitions that the disease brings about. You'll find space **at the end of this Supporting Cases section** *where you can plan your responses for these action points.*

- **What concrete plans must be put into motion at this time?**
- **Who will be in charge of implementing the plans?**
- **Do you require an action plan for medical, psychiatric, or legal assistance?**

- What professionals or organizations will need to be contacted?
- Who will be the "Point Person" in charge of coordinating care needs with professionals and handling the unforeseen and acute situations that will arise?
- What support networks need to be established to provide care and education for family members?

CASE 1 Moderate Phase

Dr. Jorgen: Husband with Alzheimer's (Dad)
Mrs. Jorgen: Wife (Mom)
Doris: Daughter of Dr. Jorgen
Daryl: Son-in-law of Dr. Jorgen

Dr. and Mrs. Jorgen moved from Delaware and have now come to live near their daughter, Doris, and her family. There has been no hint of medical or other difficulties with either of Doris's parents. Upon arrival, Dad appears to be having some difficulties performing tasks such as following through with appointments, and planning and managing financial and home chores as part of moving from out of state. As Mom relates, these are tasks that he had previously completed without difficulty. She, on the other hand, has quickly resumed her life by getting involved with church activities and the local Veterans Hospital. She is very social and spends much time with newfound friends. Dad had intentions of making friends and playing golf at the local club where their condo is located, but he is spending more time at their daughter's house with her husband, who runs his own business out of their home. Doris works full-time at a local accounting business. Their two children, both of whom are in college, are coming home for their summer vacation in three months.

Daryl, Doris's husband, has been complaining that her dad is "being bothersome," asking if there are things he could do around the home, fidgeting, constantly walking around and occasionally getting brusque when reminded that he often asks repetitive questions. Daryl reports that he appears confused when given directions to go shopping and asks two or three times a day how to get online with the computer. Doris has spoken to Daryl several times, and there appears to be no resolution. Doris is protective of her dad, especially because they strongly encouraged her parents to make the move. Now there is growing stress between her and Daryl about her dad's "attachment" to their home. Her dad's behavior is beginning to have an effect on Daryl's work production. When Dr. Jorgen speaks to his wife on the telephone, which is four to five times daily, he claims he is okay and everything is going well. Doris has spoken to her mom about their concerns: her mom responds that they are overreacting to Dad's changes and is basically unwilling to change her lifestyle. Mom does admit, after probing from Doris, that her dad was appearing to have "slowed his pace somewhat," and that was one of the reasons she had agreed to move closer to Doris and Daryl.

Yesterday, Dr. Jorgen, unbeknownst to Daryl, left the house and wandered downtown, ending up in a large mall. When Doris's mom came to pick up her husband and discovered he was not there and Daryl had no idea where he was, she exploded with fear and anger. Following a search of several hours, with the local police involved, Dr. Jorgen was found sitting on a bench at the mall. He stated that he was waiting for his wife to pick him up because that was where they agreed to meet when she finished shopping. This incident led to several serious discussions. Doris's mom was confronted about her husband's functioning prior to their coming to live closer and revealed through heavy tears that he has been failing for about seven to eight months. She had been having his friends look after and entertain him, but they eventually refused to be caregivers. Mrs. Jorgen continued to ignore the situation as long as possible, and when Doris and Daryl suggested they come closer to live, she jumped at the opportunity. Daryl was furious, and his immediate response was to state that Dr. Jorgen could no longer "be placed" with him at their home. Doris was in a difficult situation, and immediately her role in the family changed.

The grandchildren will be home in two weeks!

Changes noted in the person with dementia and the family:

In Mrs. Jorgen:
- She significantly overstates the level of independent functioning of her husband through denial and minimizing
- She shows resistance to having her life changed by her husband's continuing decline.
- The exacerbation of symptoms could be due to the recent move and loss of familiarity and routine.

In Dr. Jorgen:
- He is having difficulty keeping and following through with appointments, completing financial tasks and general banking business
- With the move near his family, he is not establishing new social relationships or participating in activities outside of the home.
- He is asking repetitive questions, wandering, showing poor focus and lapses of concentration during tasks

In Doris's family:
- Guilt/frustration of daughter and son-in-law for encouraging move and current distress

- Changes in work habits of son-in-law
- Daughter hesitant to address concerns with her mom
- Due to the lapse of acknowledgment of her husbands' decline, a family split is developing that hinders family stability with implications for future care.
- No family members directly addressing current concerns with the affected loved one

Effects and Interventions

- This is a highly emotional time for the family. The current predicament is primarily due to the lack of sharing by Mrs. Jorgen surrounding the true nature of her husband's disease. The level of trust between the families is low. This is a crucial time when openness to discuss the situation and planning for the future is most important. If Doris and Daryl are to be part of the care-giving and planning process in the future, errors of the past must be reconciled. Establishing the first line of communication at the least gets people talking without finger-pointing. This is a "what do we do now" discussion. Now is the time to involve professionals. Dr. Jorgen must be evaluated to help determine the level of care he now requires. Can he remain in his home with his wife? Does she want him to? What are the other options? What does Dr. Jorgen have to say about his dementia? What is he aware of regarding the status of his disease?

- If Mrs. Jorgen continues to minimize and deny her husband's decline, the family may become fragmented and unable to provide the necessary care and lay the important foundation for dealing with the latter phase of the disease. It is imperative that the Jorgens establish a relationship with a medical provider immediately to determine with clarity the nature and degree of Dr. Jorgen's impairment. Additionally, legal and financial consultations are in order to prepare for the inevitable costs and power of attorney that will be necessary. Following confirmation of the disease process, the family could connect with a local support group (Alzheimer's Association) to access the more informal and daily opportunities and assistance available for Dr. Jorgen and the family.

• Doris and Daryl were blindsided. They were initially excited about the prospect of having Doris's parents live nearby; based on what they knew of the situation, they could be close, with independent lives, and provide safety as Doris's folks got older. Without knowledge of her dad's present condition and not really knowing what the future holds, this change to Doris and Daryl's lives has been profound, personally and professionally. This is why it is imperative that action begins. Whether they like it or not, Doris and Daryl are involved. They must take the time to become knowledgeable so that they can make important decisions regarding personal boundaries for themselves. How involved will they become: dad-sitting, offering financial assistance, letting the folks move in at some point...? Education about dementia for Daryl and Doris would help them understand how the disease progresses and then make healthier choices about their respective roles to assist Doris's mom. The area office of the Alzheimer's Association or other local professional organization that works with the dementias could supply reading material, support group information, the latest in medication options, general treatment issues, and family intervention strategies.

• The grandchildren will be home in two weeks. At this point, considering that they are in college, there has probably been limited contact with their grandparents for some time. Does the family have them be part of the discussion about future planning, or do they become *secondary partners*? My inclination is to allow them to spend time with their grandparents and form their own observations prior to any decision-making with their parents. As adults with competing responsibilities, they have to judge for themselves, individually, what their roles could be.

In what ways is the above case different from or similar to your family situation?

_____

_____

_____

_____

_____

_____

CASE 2 Moderate Phase

Mom/Grandma: Parent with Alzheimer's
Dad/Grandpa: Her husband
Bonnie: Daughter
Aiden & Louie: Grandchildren

Mom and Dad live about five hours away, and their daughter, Bonnie, gets to see them about every three months. They are retired and have had active lives. Over the past year, their once weekly telephone conversations have gotten shorter and Mom spends less time talking with the grandchildren. There are times when she has a reason for not talking to them at all. Over the past month, Mom has called several times asking who this is, not remembering she called, or misdialing Bonnie's number. After several "weird" questions, she regains her composure and has a pleasant, although short, conversation. There have been several phone calls in which she asked Bonnie questions about what had happened to old papers and bankbooks from former accounts. Other times she has suggested that someone had been stealing and selling her jewelry and other personal items. Recently, while Dad was on the telephone talking to one of her children, Bonnie could hear her mom yelling in the background that he had stolen her diamond ring and probably gave it to another woman.

Bonnie's father has downplayed Mom's behaviors although acknowledging that she is more moody and forgetful and less patient than in the past. Bonnie has suggested to her dad several times that they visit for a long weekend or that she go to visit them, but her offers have been declined because of "other plans." Bonnie and her husband are getting worried that there may be something medically wrong that her folks are not sharing. Last week was Aiden's eighth birthday. Bonnie's mom has never failed to call on anyone's birthday or special event regarding the children. After waiting two days, Bonnie called her mom and was told she was lying. Her mom stated that she had called and spoken to Louie (Bonnie's other child). When Bonnie disputed her recollection, her mom started yelling at her that she was just like her father and abruptly hung up the telephone. She refused to answer the phone when Bonnie called back. When Bonnie spoke to her dad later that evening, he stated that he did not know that she had called and said that her mom was having a bad day and not feeling well. Bonnie decided that she had to go visit and find out what was going on. She told her husband that it was wise for the family to not go at this time because of the odd manner of things. He agreed and she set off to visit her folks alone. Bonnie decided not to call prior to the visit and that if something was wrong, this was the best way to discover the truth.

When she arrived at their home, she rang the doorbell, even though she had a key. Her mom answered through the door. With the door closed, Bonnie told her who it was. Mom said, "My daughter does not live here and you should leave." Bonnie tried to explain that she *was* her daughter but got vague indistinguishable responses. As she was about to use the key, she heard her father asking her mom what was going on, and Mom said that someone was trying to break in. Bonnie called through the door, and he eventually opened it to see it was her. Her mom had left the area and gone to her room. When Bonnie entered the house, things were a mess, with clothes and clutter all around. The house smelled of spoiled food and Dad looked ragged. After telling him why she was there, she could see tears in his eyes. There were also bruises up and down both of his arms.

Changes noted in the person with dementia and the family:

In Mom:
- Changed communication patterns: she is less talkative, has confused rambling conversations, misunderstands messages
- High level of disorientation to ongoing routine events and working memory errors
- Increased paranoia and agitation, and distrust of her husband
- Increased display of verbal and physical anger
- Isolation from family

In Dad:
- Complicity in covering up the progress of the disease
- Poor safety and judgment to maintain the status quo
- Physical abuse by his wife

Effects and Interventions

- People who enter the moderate phase of Alzheimer's begin to *lose or distort information* that they already know, and more rapidly forget or fail to retain most new information. The confusion from Mom over her daughter's references is not surprising. Monthly visits and weekly telephone conversations are not going to keep her active memories current. Abstract thought, catching references, and visualizing what is not in front of her are becoming difficult and frustrating for Mom. Verbal cueing could help, but it can't sustain her memory without constant reminders, unless the cues are visual and referenced routinely. Additionally, what is discussed on the telephone will be lost or distorted. For example, Bonnie might suggest that she is thinking of taking a ride up to see her mom and dad in a few days, and the next morning Mom could translate the information into "I have to clean the house now because Bonnie will be here any minute."

• Dad has been attempting to address immediate needs on a daily basis for Mom. He is unable to keep up with providing safety and planning for himself or his wife. There could be several reasons, including ones stated in earlier parts of the book regarding shame, secrecy, guilt, and denial. He has suffered greatly to date, and the longer he isolates the situation the greater the difficulty in seeking assistance, prolonging lack of safety and allowing his wife to avoid accepting outside assistance in any form. Bonnie's discovery of the situation has the potential to begin a healthier family course of action that will include social and professional interventions.

• Mom's cognitive losses are becoming widespread, including poor retention of new information (loss of short-term memory) and distortion of remote memory (calling her grandson by his brother's name). There is confusion in processing information, and possibly she is experiencing paranoid delusions. She is accusatory and agitated and is isolating herself. The description of the house when Bonnie comes to visit lets us see that hygiene, both general and personal, has become a major problem.

• So what next? Following the initial shock, Bonnie has several immediate and important discussions to have and decisions to make. Caught by the immediacy of the situation, Dad may be temporarily amenable to necessary changes. I suspect that after he "unloads" his misery to Bonnie, he will want to pull back from any significant changes. The emotional release and sharing with Bonnie will afford him the potential to pull together more energy and continue as is. This position will be strongly supported by Mom, who is suspicious of any change and has lost the ability to know what is best for her. Bonnie must help Dad decide priorities: Mom's safety, Dad's safety, the immediate need for outside assistance (medical, psychological, and legal intervention). The key to moving forward with the proper care will be Bonnie's ability to "get Dad on board." Once he understands the critical nature of the situation and frees himself from whatever is binding him, together he and Bonnie can provide the health care for Mom. There is a strong possibility that Mom will fight against any proposed changes.

• An equally important piece that Bonnie must address includes bringing her family up to date with the present functioning of her mom. If her folks are able to remain in their household with the proper assistance, the burden will fall less on Bonnie at this time. If her mom is no longer able to be at home safely, other placement arrangements must be considered, and Bonnie and husband have important decisions concerning their possible financial and time commitment. If there is the thought that Grandma and Grandpa should live with Bonnie's family, it should be a decision made following long thought and planning. At this time, Bonnie must take this *opportunity* with her young children to explain the changes they will see in Grandma the next time they see her. Explaining may be a temporary fix until there is face to face contact. At that time, the children will require more time and resources (books, coaching) to help them adjust. This family is behind the curve in exercising a plan for the acute and longer term solutions. Bonnie can anticipate that ANY changes in the daily life of her parents will be met with resistance and possibly a more rapid decline in her mom's status.

In what ways is the above case example different from or similar to your family situation?

_____

_____

_____

_____

_____

_____

CASE 3 Moderate Phase

Becky: Wife with Alzheimer's
Hayes: Husband

Becky has been living in a group home for the past three years. Over the prior two months, her ability to care for her daily needs has diminished to the point of requiring assistance for toileting, completion of dressing herself, and prevention from wandering away from the home into the busier part of town. While she remains able to request her needs and carry on *surface social communication,* her retention of information and reasoning skills are noticeably limited in detail, with increased word loss. Becky has begun demanding to be taken home by her husband, Hayes. Hayes has been spending much time with Becky, attempting to soothe her anger by taking her out to dinner, taking her home for the afternoon and anything he can think of to permit her to stay at the group home. It has not worked. When Hayes does take her home, she wanders around the home, unable to sit still, moving items around—and in less than an hour she is ready to leave.

With the increase in her dementia symptoms, the group home has determined she is no longer able to safely reside there, and she has been given a thirty-day notice to leave. The options are to go to a skilled nursing facility (SNF) or back home with Hayes. When Hayes attempts to discuss this with Becky, she clearly states, "I want to go home." Hayes has explained to Becky a number of reasons why she could not return home, but Becky denies every reason and remains adamant she can care for herself. Hayes has been married to

Becky for thirteen years. Becky has two adult children from her first marriage, and they have been available for telephone discussion only. They appear to be satisfied with how Hayes is managing the situation and do not have the finances to be present for direct care and consultation. Hayes is highly emotional and spends much time in tears and frustrated, not socializing with friends and making almost daily visits to the group home. Becky has good moments when she loves, answers questions clearly, appears insightful, and socializes well. Unfortunately, these times are far outnumbered by the difficult, anxious, and angry times, with Becky unable to manage her feelings and think clearly.

Hayes has consulted with Becky's primary care physician and asked him to help by telling Becky she is not able to return home and she needs to be in assisted living. The physician suggests maybe he could try having her home for a short period to see if she will be convinced she cannot be there. He has agreed to have Becky on medication for her anxiety and cognitive loss. As the pressure mounts on Hayes to make an informed, clear decision regarding Becky's placement, he further isolates himself, which increases his depressive symptoms and feelings of failure as a husband.

Changes noted in the person with dementia and the family:

Becky:
- Requires routine assistance to maintain proper hygiene.
- Shows markedly diminished retention of information and reasoning skills, with increased word loss
- Wanders without purpose and safety awareness

- Has unpredictable mood changes with increase in verbal anger and physical agitation
- Lacks the insight to appreciate the changes taking place and how these changes affect those around them.
- Exhibits poor recognition of safety for self
- Has poor understanding of how her behavior affects Hayes
- Shows increasingly poor insight and judgment as to her level of functioning

Hayes:
- Attempts to provide the best possible care without acceptance from his loved one, which causes increasing depressive episodes
- Struggles with providing a secure safe environment for Becky and the ongoing grief and emotional consequences of a more secure environment for his wife
- Is withdrawing from social support and balanced self-care
- Has increased stress over the changes in Becky's condition
- Increased time allotted to care-giving and soothing Becky when she is agitated or angry

Effects and Interventions

• Becky's condition has changed. Her ability to maintain herself at the group home is tenuous and becoming dangerous to herself and other residents. Wandering has become a problem and Becky requires a wander guard or a facility alert system to prevent her from leaving the grounds. The unpredictability of her behaviors also creates a safety issue. With the increasing loss of judgment, reasoning skills, and insight to her actions, her decision-making abilities diminish and therefore her independence must be curtailed by firmer restrictions. Group homes are generally not equipped to work with patients who have behavioral unpredictability and wandering potential such as Becky has.

•   Hayes feels like he is alone in his endeavors to assist Becky and make the correct decisions for her safety. Certainly, with the limited help from Becky's daughters, much of the decision-making weight falls on him. Hopefully, legal documents, including advanced directives, power of attorney, and financial arrangements have been completed. If not, it is urgent that he set up the proper paperwork to take full control of Becky's care. As we know, family *from away,* who have previously been unavailable for assistance, can attempt to become players at any time. In this situation one must consider that Becky's daughters are from her previous marriage and their thinking could be that they have the primary duty to care for Mom now that she is unable to care for herself. This situation could have financial implications and the sense that daughters must protect their mother.

•   Hayes requires emotional and possibly, legal assistance. He is on an emotional roller coaster, easily swayed by his love for Becky, by guilt and grieving. I would strongly recommend Hayes begin counseling with a professional who is knowledgeable about these situations and can help him sort out the complicated emotional and practical decisions he must undertake. Additionally, Hayes does not appear to be using his personal and social support system. Many communities have local chapters of the Alzheimer's Association, which can provide a viable support group. This is the time when a primary caregiver may suffer great personal damage. Making a difficult decision, like having your spouse committed into a skilled nursing facility could bring on feelings of failure and guilt, which could interfere with a healthy decision-making process.

• **No matter how hard she tries, Becky may not be able to do any better.** Hayes wants desperately to consider Becky's needs but is unable to satisfy her. She cannot appreciate the caring and reasons behind his recommendations. Logically, he recognizes her best interests lie in a more secure environment but emotionally he is grieving and not able to complete the task. Becky is making demands on her husband, the group home, and anyone that may come in contact with her. This is not uncommon at this point. Feeling frustrated and not understanding why but knowing something is wrong, people with Alzheimer's search for answers but just can't figure out what they need, how to get it, or when they have it. There is a growing, frightening emptiness. **They are searching, for what they do not know, and whatever others suggest does not satisfy.** I believe this is connected to the larger degree of confusion and emptiness later in the disease when a person attempts to fill purpose and understanding with remote memory, which remains somewhat intact (although distorted by sequence and content) for a longer period of time.

• It is a good time for Hayes to attempt to meet with Becky's daughters. They may not want to be actively involved and have remained distant because they fear Hayes calling on them to increase their time commitment. We are not certain what the relationship was historically between Becky and her daughters and there may be clear reasons for their distance. They may be frightened, angry or in a state of denial. It is possible that Hayes does not know. Now is the time to find out. Hayes could simplify any possible tension and answer any questions by approaching them. He could clarify his role, his limitations, what he foresees for the future and what expectations, if any, he has of her daughters. Granted, as Becky's condition worsens, the daughters may react in unpredictable ways, yet this is a starting point for outlining family care.

• Hayes must find medical help that will provide sound, knowledgeable assistance. At this point in the disease process, there are a number of considerations for medical care. As behavior and cognition diminish, increased use of medication becomes necessary as does the potential treatment for co-existing psychiatric problems and other acute medical conditions or the exacerbation of chronic ills. If Becky is already on medications, compatibility with new medications is a concern. Becky is looking at a transition to a new living arrangement. This could cause a temporary spike in confusion and general agitation. Proper medications could ease this transition.

In what ways is the above case example different from or similar to your family situation?

_____

_____

_____

_____

_____

CASE 4 Moderate Phase

This case represents the continuation of Case 4, Early Phase

Sam: Husband with Alzheimer's Lucille: Wife
Caitlyn: Adult daughter   Janae: Adult daughter

A year and a half has passed since the description of the early phase of this case. Sam and Lucille continue to live in their home with one daughter and family nearby and another downstate. Lucille has given up her part-time job as a food taster to be at home with Sam. Sam is not getting out of the house much anymore. He spends time lounging in his recliner watching television and napping during the day. Other times he wanders around the home as Lucille attempts to direct him in chores he rarely accomplishes. Sam starts a small project but comes to find Lucille with questions about what he is supposed to do or why he is doing it. Other times she finds him either asleep in his chair or fidgeting with something else. More than a few times, he has unexpectedly starting yelling at Lucille when he could not understand what she wanted of him or blamed her for his errors. Nobody knows about the times he lashed out at her with his open hand or picked up a nearby object and threatened to hit her with it. Sam can follow his simple daily routine most of the time, but Lucille has awakened several times recently very early in the morning with Sam standing above her fully dressed and "ready for work." Sam has forgotten the names of their grandchildren, and when they visit, which has become rare, he does not interact alone with them. When their daughter Caitlyn and her husband come over to the house, more often than not, the children do not accompany them. Visits are shorter, with fewer activities connected to their meals together.

Last week, their other daughter, Janae, who lives downstate, made a surprise visit to their home. Her mom answered the door with red teary eyes, and her dad was yelling from their bedroom. Her dad came out of the bedroom with a shoe in his hand looking for her mom. Janae yelled at her dad and he stopped, looked at them and slowly walked back into the bedroom. Lucille burst into tears and confessed to Janae how terrible things had become. After talking to her mother for over an hour and finding out that Caitlyn did not know what was going on either, she became angry and attempted to dictate what was to happen. She called her sister and began ranting on the telephone about what she walked in on, accusing her of not caring for their mother and ignoring the dire situation. Janae hung up on Caitlyn, and so began the next phase of family interaction.

Changes noted in the person with dementia and the family:

In Sam:
- Increased emotional outbursts and aggressive behavior
- Increase in wandering without purpose
- Decrease in social interactions
- Short attention span, poor retention of new information
- Decreased insight, judgment, and reasoning
- Highly reactive and confused in high stimulus situations
- Has had several falls

- Forgetting the names of objects and using the wrong word in a given context

In Lucille:
- Does not share Sam's cognitive loss with her daughters or the doctor when he goes for medical checkups.
- Will not take Sam with her to the supermarket or any busy stores
- Has accepted Sam's deteriorating cognitive and behavioral changes and the need to take on increasing caregiver responsibilities

In Caitlyn:
- Has changed the visitation pattern with her mom and dad; often not bringing their children to visit
- Poor communication with Janae as to how the disease and its effects have progressed

In Janae:
- Caught off guard by the poor situation when she made a surprise visit to her parents
- Wants to "take over" the care and has great anger at her sister for 'letting things get to this point'.

Effects and Interventions

- Sam appears to have settled in to a safer, easier routine to accommodate for his increasing decline in cognitive clarity. He spends increased time at home alone with Lucille, rests when he wants, and generally lives a life with little change or surprise, where the routine is very familiar. This lifestyle is preferred for someone in his overall state of decline. Considering his cognitive losses, he feels safer and is not confronted with many decisions regarding daily routine. When Sam is challenged by Lucille or a change in the environment, he becomes agitated and aggressive or withdraws into sleep (as self-protection).

• Sam does not readily engage the rest of the family. More importantly, the family has resigned themselves to not engaging with Sam. This may or may not be on a fully conscious level, but their lack of physical and mental connection is hurting Sam and them. This is not an unusual response for some family members; but considering that there is another sibling, in addition to the one who lives nearby and can thus be in regular contact, the levels of participation in care varies. As a result, there is greater need to involve all members of the family. Another consideration may be the reason(s) some family members would tend to withdraw from participating in the situation (family history, finances...). It is during this phase of the disease that intimate contact and familiarity are essential to keep people with Alzheimer's challenged to maintain whatever functioning they have left. **This is generally not the "*provide comfort only*" phase.**

• Sam is not able to complete tasks that require multiple steps or a prolonged period of time to complete. It is vital for Lucille to develop tasks for him that he is able to complete and that make him feel successful. Sam's sense of success is becoming increasingly based upon concrete observable ends, so tasks should require less time to finish, with fewer separate steps to complete with the result clearly observable for Sam to understand. With multiple steps and insight required

113

to understand the utility of the project, Sam will invariably become increasingly disheartened, confused, and agitated. Structure in Sam's daily home life with time for simple computer games, reminiscence activities and day-care at a local facility could help to maintain Sam's functional level for extended periods.

• I am concerned with Lucille's approach to Sam. She appears willing to sacrifice her own well-being while hiding Sam's decline. This poses danger for both of them and for the rest of the family. Lucille is becoming the accepted target of Sam's confusion and increasing violence. Lucille's poor judgment is in thinking that she can somehow limit Sam's decline or absorb his hostility to keep him *better longer,* or protect herself from her acceptance of loss. Lucille may feel somehow responsible for Sam's decline and does not want to *burden the rest of the family.* This may be an old family dynamic that her children have bought into and not paid close attention to since Sam's decline.

• There are several immediate necessary adjustments in care that Lucille must initiate. Sam will require a medical checkup to determine any changes in his medical status and the potential for any coexisting psychiatric conditions (depression, anxiety disorder, etc.). There may be need to start or review medication use for agitation, aggressiveness, or the level of cognitive decline. Lucille could benefit from the assistance of a support group or individual counseling to develop coping strategies for Sam's behavior changes and cognitive decline. As stated above, Sam could continue to benefit from appropriate structured cognitive challenges and social contact. Now that the *door has been opened* with her daughters, the time is appropriate for the family to come together and develop plans for current and future concerns. There must be an open "let's put it all on the table" discussion that will involve family, professionals, and any potential caregiver involvement (in-home or residential).

• Blame is easy at this time. Mom has been protecting and secretive about Dad's decline, and neither daughter has paid the attention necessary to uncover the current situation. I continue to stress how *it is urgent for the family to remain focused in the present and not get caught up in historical family dynamics that could cloud the best decisions for present actions and future planning.* Clarifying roles and responsibilities for each member of the family will increase the communication and relieve the sense of overwhelming individual burden. It will also enable each family member to give to Sam the positive attention, care, and loving relationships he can still accept and appreciate.

• Grandchildren in the family will reconnect with Sam if given the proper tools and guidance. They are grieving the change in relationship with their grandfather, and they continue to have much to offer. It is imperative that they be apprised of the current situation and given active ways they can feel helpful and part of the family plan. Sam may be reluctant at first to reengage the grandchildren, so it is important to develop ways that are not threatening and are fun for Sam and the grandchildren. Younger children can draw, look at photos, and practice reading with Sam. Older children and teens can take walks, assist with simple projects, watch television, and listen and discuss with Sam as he talks about his earlier life.

In what ways is the above case different from or similar to your family situation?

_____

_____

_____

_____

_____

_____

CASE 5 Moderate Phase

Sophia: Alzheimer's disease   Sol: Husband
Allan: Oldest son   Logan: Youngest son
Wendy: Daughter   Tyquan: Grandchild

Sol and Sophia have lived in the same town for the past 18 years and have many friends and social ties. Two years ago they moved into an assisted living arrangement when Sophia was first diagnosed with Alzheimer's disease. Sophia displayed a number of the symptoms found in the earlier phase of the disease, while still maintaining much of her independent persona. She has now given up driving and going for walks or to town by herself. Over the past several months, Sophia has shown a decline in her cognitive abilities, with an increase in emotional and behavioral unpredictability including periods of sitting for hours isolated in her room and, at other times, pacing without purpose or destination. There have been several recent episodes of aimlessly wandering at night in the common areas of the complex. Some mornings, Sophia awakens Sol stating that she needs him to drive her to work or she will be late and possibly fired from her job. Earlier in her life, Sophia had been a wonderful cook, and now she forgets how to turn the oven on or off. One time she left a dish towel on the burner she thought she turned off; the resulting fire was contained. Last week, she got lost in their complex and walked into another apartment extremely confused and thinking that strangers were in her apartment.

Their three children live out of state and had been kept up to date with their mom's disease process—that is, until her recent decline. In earlier years they were a close family; they remain in regular contact, and over the past ten years, each child has had the opportunity to have the family visit over the Christmas holiday. This past October, Dad called, saying that they would not be joining the family this year and provided no further information. Allan, the oldest, whose house they were all to come to this year, notified the others. They made a plan for Logan, the youngest, to go to their parent's apartment and escort them to Allan's home. Sol protested, but after being told the children and families would come to visit them, agreed to visit at Allan's home for three days.

The three days turned out to be a very stressful time for the entire family. Sol and Sophia stayed with Allan and his family in their large home. The other children and their families stayed at a local motel. By the first evening, Sophia had grown quite agitated when she could not find her room. She wandered around the home until Sol would escort her to their bedroom and stay there with her. This happened each evening. The grandchildren, who were elementary school age, could not understand why Grandma could not remember their names. When they asked her to read with them, she would stay for a few minutes then arise and make herself busy. Their daughter, Wendy, took her mother shopping one afternoon and had great difficulty in stores with her wandering and continually asking for Sol. On the second day, while Sophia was napping, the children finally had the opportunity to talk with their father about the dramatic changes in Mom. On the last night at dinner, Logan's four-year-old son, Tyquan, fell and started to cry. Sophia yelled out, "Stop that child from crying!" Sol and Sophia were driven to the airport the next day and returned to their apartment in the assisted living complex.

Changes noted in person with dementia and the family:

In Sophia:
- Having alternate periods of depressive and anxious signs
- Pacing in the apartment (especially at night) and aimlessly wandering around the complex
- Insisting to spouse that she had to leave for scheduled appointments and meetings in town (delusions)
- Experiencing a change in sleeping habits
- Having difficulty with proper use of appliances
- Not remembering the names of their close friends or grandchildren
- Getting lost in familiar places
- Becoming confused when visiting family and staying in an unfamiliar environment
- Showing lowered tolerance for change and environmental stimulation

In the family:
- Sol has done well to downsize the couple's living arrangements and simplify their daily lives to accommodate for the disease changes
- Sol has not shared his wife's dramatic decline, and the children were unprepared when their parents visited
- Sons and daughter were initially unable to accept the changes in their mother

- Grandchildren cannot understand why their grand-mother doesn't remember their names and spends limited time with them

Effects and Interventions

- It appears easy to discern from the changes noted in this case that Sophia has progressed to the moderate phase of the disease. Her loss of general orientation and limited ability to use appliances safely signal that she requires full-time care and watchfulness. Distortion and possibly delusions surround her thought processes, and her behavioral routine is not stable or predictable. What we do not know at this time is whether Sol recognizes that these changes in Sophia's presentation warrant another change in their lifestyle. As Sol becomes a full time caregiver, other things may suffer, including his independence. Does Sophia require a new level of care management with the arrangement for in-home care? Or does she need the next level, with restrictions to the environment (assisted living or group home)?

- Why did Sol decide to go on the vacation? Did he know that it was not a good idea for Sophia to travel at this time? Was his decision based on obliging the family, or not wanting them to witness what was happening in their apartment? If Sophia's condition was clearly communicated and understood by the children, there probably would not have been so much pressure and possibly different holiday arrangements. Family routines are difficult to alter, and accommodations for three generations can be taxing. That is why open family communication is essential for safe planning. Generally any permanent changes in the immediate environment, at this phase of the disease, would take several weeks at minimum for adjustment. A potential benefit of this situation is how the children witness, firsthand, their mom's decline and can choose to become more involved in her care and begin the arduous task of planning.

• This raises another question. Has Sol consulted with a medical or behavioral health professional about the changes over the past few months? Did he discuss the potential of travel for Sophia? If there was consultation, he and the children would have been prepared for the difficulties that confronted them at their son's home and would not have been surprised by her loss of cognitive orientation and behaviors. If there was no consultation, why not? This may be an indication of Sol's continuing denial or minimizing of Sophia's declining condition. The family visit may help to jump-start the action required to secure the proper level of safety and care for Sophia. This family appears to be intimately involved and wants to remain in the picture.

• Addressing the grandchildren is important at this point. If Grandma's telephone and visiting time has already been limited, then the older ones would be aware of the changes. They may not have asked questions but may be passively accepting less interaction. Following this latest visit, however, full discussions are necessary. Younger children think in concrete terms and primarily pay attention to the immediate situation—in this case, Grandma's reticence to engage and spend time with them. The holiday time is special and, with their parents, the children have been happily anticipating the arrival of their grandparents. If the adults of the house are tense and requesting the children to "behave," the children may disappear or feel blamed for *being children*. Getting through these few days requires patience for everyone. Upon the conclusion of the visit, the parents must continue the education about Alzheimer's so that the grandchildren can understand and can be part of the continuing care.

In what ways is the above case different from or similar to your family situation?

_____

_____

_____

_____

_____

CREATING AN ACTION PLAN

Now that you have read the cases illustrating the challenges of this phase of Alzheimer's disease, you may fill in the spaces after the following action items. I hope this can serve as a starting point to develop a plan for how you will move through the transitions that the disease brings about.

What concrete plans must be put into motion at this time?

_____

_____

_____

_____

Who will be in charge of implementing the plans?

_____

_____

_____

_____

Do you require an action plan for medical, psychiatric, or legal assistance?

_____

_____

_____

_____

What professionals or organizations will need to be contacted?

_____

_____

_____

_____

Who will be the "Point Person" in charge of coordinating care needs with professionals and handling the unforeseen and acute situations that will arise?

_____

_____

_____

_____

What support networks need to be established to provide care and education for family members?

_____

_____

_____

_____

Chapter 3

Alzheimer's Dementia: Advanced Phase

"My wife is fading away like an old photograph;
I am losing her—she is a child dressed as a woman"
Kurt, a spouse

Segment One:
Overview

The advanced phase of Alzheimer's disease, sometimes referred to as the *comfort phase,* presents a different set of circumstances, ones that will test the mettle of the family. The affected loved one is no longer tactically involved in the decision-making process, and the full burden of decision-making and daily care falls upon the holder of the power of attorney and/or the family. Wherever the person with Alzheimer's is living at this time, the involved family is overworked and underprepared for the intensity of their path. In the beginning segment of this phase, the person may still be in their home, or in the family's home, receiving in-home daily care through an outside source or in combination with family support. For affected loved ones still in the home, with luck their behaviors have been manageable to this point, and the family is highly united in their desire to provide their loved one with as comfortable a transition as possible. **Transition to a secure environment should be strongly considered in this phase of the disease.** No longer is the person with Alzheimer's predictable or safe to self or others; he or she requires assistance with Activities of Daily Living (ADLs) and not able to follow most verbal directions or written cues. Hopefully, the necessary legal, financial, and medical paperwork is completed and in order. Those who decide to ignore the inevitable downward slide will be scrambling to find a placement for the loved one, possibly not of their choosing, as their loved one's behavior and general medical condition has declined severely enough to require a specialized unit designed for behaviorally challenged people.

It is urgent to recognize the balance between the best possible safety and comfort for your loved one, and the safety and health of the family.

By this time most people suffering from Alzheimer's disease are in an assisted living facility, group home, or skilled nursing facility. This could depend on several combinations of factors:

- The financial status of the impaired or family
- The proximity and availability of family for assisting in care
- Marital status of the impaired and health of the significant other
- Degree of cognitive and/or behavioral decline
- Mitigating medical or psychiatric problems

When the loved one goes into any type of institution, expect to feel many mixed emotions—guilt and a sense of failure; you will cry, feel relief, feel guilty because you feel relieved and now have more time for yourself and family. Unfortunately, there are situations when the family cannot afford the costs of having a loved one enter a care facility. Accessing state or federal funding programs may be an alternative. These programs are based primarily on income and availability. Guidelines vary between states and should be examined carefully.

Most notably and, probably, most difficult for the family to work with is the loss of cognitive awareness and general orientation of the person with Alzheimer's. I will discuss in further detail the significant effects these changes have on children and teenagers, but for now I will present some of the more general debilitating transformations.

Early in this phase, people with Alzheimer's lose insight, judgment, and reasoning. This is important because they lose their ability to get meaning from many questions and statements. If you say it is raining, they do not have the insight to understand that when they go outdoors, they will need raingear. Judgment helps us make decisions to decide between choices that appear similar but have subtle differences. We can weigh the implications and project results of whichever choice we make. Reasoning is another skill that assists in our ability to look at options and consider the alternatives for best results. Immediate and recent memory at this phase is quite poor, and retention of history is sketchy and occurs with distortion.

Do not ask the person with Alzheimer's if he or she knows who you are or what your name is. Ask questions only if they are relevant to care and safety. Make eye contact, use few words and talk slowly.

At this point the ability to plan, organize, and provide any kind of problem-solving is greatly diminished for the person with

Alzheimer's. Concentration is poor, with increased word loss and general speech impairment. There may be an increase in delusions (distortion of thoughts), which are caused by a lack of orientation, disorganized thinking patterns, or triggers from the environment that are often confusing. Delusions can trigger unpredictable mood changes, paranoia, acute distress, crying, fear, or confusion. Behaviorally, people with Alzheimer's disease at this phase have an increase in fall risk, striking out, impulsive responses, and problems with bathing, eating, and incontinence.

During this time, tasks that appear simple to us are too complex for those with dementia, and they require assistance or leadership. For example, brushing teeth or getting dressed must be broken down into simple sequential steps. Continuing modification of tasks helps those with dementia be part of the process and eases frustration. At this point in the disease process, a person will have great difficulty or not be able to learn new tasks and should only focus on already learned routines. It is imperative to use cueing for requests, as even the simplest routines are often too confusing for the person to navigate (for example, how to put on a button down shirt). There is greater distortion of the senses, and shadows, coloring, textures, contrasts, and similarities (all doors look the same) cause greater confusion, agitation, and resistance.

As this phase of the disease progresses, the person with Alzheimer's has lost the ability to communicate in sentences and may spontaneously speak independent words (either making sense or not). Their words may be in response to questions, needs, changes in the environment, or this may occur in reaction to delusions and/or hallucinations. There remains a sense of familiarity with some loved ones (facial or voice familiarity but not name or relationship). People in this phase are oriented to themselves and possibly general surroundings; they experience their lives in the immediate, acting on internal urges and environmental stimulation (which they are drawn to but do not understand). Medications may be increased which can cause drowsiness and other physical or mental changes that further hinder clarity.

Try as they may, people with these symptoms of Alzheimer's remain primarily oriented only to themselves. They lose the ability to identify, enjoy, and embrace family members and their love as the family would wish. I have found that younger children begin to accept these realities before teens and adults. Maybe it is because of their naiveté and innocence, maybe because their relationship does not have the longer history, or because they are more inclined to realize that their grandparent is *no longer with them.*

People with this advanced degree of dementia are able to:

- Move body parts in response to internal or external stimuli
- Move gaze to follow bright color contrasts
- Increase alertness to familiar auditory input
- Hold and use objects of daily use placed in the hand
- Strike out to protect themselves when startled
- Feed self if given hand-over-hand assistance
- Sit in fully supported chair for brief periods during alert times

They function best when they are given:

- Visual presentation before tactile contact
- Gentle, slow massage or handling
- Highly structured, single presentation sensory stimulation (auditory, visual, tactile)
- Gentle swaddling to help calm them
- Reduction in sudden and loud noises
- Total assistance with self-care

Predominant areas of decline and loss include:

- Memory: retention of information and working memory severely impaired
- Language loss: aphasia, loss of fluency; impairment ranging from inability to form complete sentences to use of incompatible words (word salad) to complete loss of speech—this impairment decreases the ability to express pain or desires
- Visual-spatial skills, spatial disorientation, abstract reasoning
- Calculation ability
- Motor system deficits: restlessness and pacing; high fall risk (loss of balance and forgetting how to walk); generalized body rigidity
- Personality changes: from indifference or irritability to no clear personality traits available
- Psychiatric features: delusions and other co-existing conditions in some
- Need for full ADL care
- The brain appears not to tell the body what to do
- Ability to control behavior and impulsive movement declines (striking out); the person with Alzheimer's may appear to be disinhibited

- Loss of hearing and/or sight exacerbate confusion

Segment Two:
Family Considerations

Children and Teens

- Younger children may want to spend less time visiting their grandparent as the grandparent becomes unable to talk to or acknowledge the child.
- Younger children may continue to question why this is happening to their grandparent and may feel some sense of responsibility.
- If Grandma or Grandpa was living with the family, children may experience sleep disturbance or inappropriate school behavior or academic changes when the grandparent moves into a facility.
- Children may become easily frightened by the new environment their grandparent has been placed in, focusing on behaviors or vocal emanations of others in the facility.
- In some facilities, visitation may be limited to one or two people at a time, or even adults only.
- Children may have further questions about why the grandparent does not recognize or acknowledge them; they may observe frightening behavior from their grandparent or hear words that make no sense.
- Questions regarding any changes in the family behavior or routine will continue. Younger children may even question why they, or you, have to go visit the grandparent.
- Some children will become increasingly protective of their grandparent and want to hold them. Children's

sudden movements may frighten their grandparent and produce a protective or violent reaction.

- Young children may ask a question such as why medications or doctors can't make Grandpa better and why does my grandpa need to be here with all these weird people.
- Prior to any visitation to a skilled nursing facility or any similar environment, parents must *educate their younger children.*
- It would be wise for children to bring *gifts* for their grandparent—something simple, colorful, and with a special meaning to the child to keep the established bond with their grandparent.
- Teens will tend to want to spend less time with visitations. They may challenge parents on the placement or the care provided, attempting to be protective to help their sense of helplessness in this situation. It is important for parents to spend time openly discussing the placement in an adult manner. Talk about why this option was taken and reinforce the idea of best comfort care for their grandparent.
- Teens will continue to benefit from someone (probably not a family member) to talk to about the changes—a spiritual guide, a friend, or another adult.
- Teens and children will continue to benefit from *special* time with parent(s).
- Teens may experience relief and appear uncaring that their grandparent is in a facility, especially if the grandparent was in their home and they had *extra* responsibilities that they no longer have.

Family Interaction

- Difficult decisions for the family are plentiful concerning comfort care, finances, medical care appropriateness, and end of life.
- Grief becomes a major ingredient in the decision-making process. Remember that each generation will grieve differently.
- The focus of family time changes with increasing *management* of care by the institution, and the parents' loss of their parent.
- Parents will need to pay close attention to their children's sleep habits, social activities, and academic lives.
- It is important to set aside time to talk to children and teens about their worst fears.
- As Grandma loses her identity and connection to members of the family, discussing these changes becomes important for the health of the children and parents.
- Input from family members not previously involved may start up when it comes to comfort measures and life/death decisions.
- Denial, minimizing, fear, fatigue, and sorrow will be spontaneous for the family members.
- Caregiver burnout may increase, especially with spouses, as they believe that they can provide the best care or that their loved one *needs them to be at the institution for hours each day.*
- Guilt surrounding the decision for placement is high, especially if a parent or grandparent has this dreaded disease.

Segment Three:
Accommodations for Care

As in the previous overview segments (for the early and moderate phases), I will review the seven ongoing themes to show the numerous changes taking place in the functioning and the corresponding effects on the family.

1. **Safety:** This is a priority during the advanced phase. In the earlier phases, the person with Alzheimer's is probably ambulating independently or with a walker, unless there is a medical condition compromising their walking ability. But now, when walking, gait is poor; the affected person is prone to stumbling. With poor concentration and easy distraction by noise or voices of others, he or she will: not observe objects on the ground, misjudge distance and width, begin to shuffle and miss rises or changes in floor coverings and surface. By this time, handling electronics, machinery, child care, and any multi-step task is dangerous and well beyond the abilities of the person with Alzheimer's. **The affected loved one living in the family home, or with the spouse, should not be left alone.** In the case of an emergency, the affected person could not respond with the speed and efficiency necessary to deal with the crisis at hand. Later during this phase, the person with Alzheimer's is in a 24/7 care environment with trained staff to watch and provide the necessary ongoing safety. The environments of these specialized facilities cater to the potential dangers that may befall the Alzheimer's patient, although there is no sure way to eliminate all danger. Impulsive and disinhibited behavior coupled with the

lack of rational thought produces potential danger at every moment. For those with increased behavior complications, safety for themselves and others becomes *the* primary goal of professional staff.

2. **Flow of Communication:** By this time, "flow of communication" may not occur. At first there may be structure to spoken sentences, but with distortion and word loss, much of what is said could be nonsensical, or the combination of several thoughts may be rolled into one statement. As mentioned above, the cognitive distortions and loss make what is said unreliable and challenging to respond to. Requests are made and changed, charges are levied, and frustration grows and tempers flare. Caregivers, spouse, and family members lose tolerance, repeat themselves often, and begin to ignore the person with Alzheimer's. It is not unusual for the affected loved one to become fixated on certain topics and repeat requests or accusations even though answers are given. The affected person's ability to absorb and interpret the information is lost! Discovering family closeness and cooperation during care for their loved one has great benefit for the family members and the affected. The necessary role changes can produce new and renewed caring and respect in a once fragmented family system. Conversely, this kind of change and associated pressures, as stated earlier, can tear the family apart, making care for their loved one and each other extremely difficult.

3. **Attention to medical, legal, and social concerns:** Planning for your loved one with dementia means *plan-*

ning for the coming days, hours, or minutes. Attempting to coordinate care-giving along with appointments for all members of the family is a daunting task when a family member with Alzheimer's remains in the family home. Structuring care-giving, appointments and others' schedules around the affected loved one is the order of the day for those who are living with family. Travel becomes an elaborate affair requiring careful planning and more time than you think. People with Alzheimer's are increasingly fearful of any transition, change in the environment, and requests that they see "new" people. Scheduling appointments with professionals is difficult, because caregivers must pay attention to the time of day, eating and elimination schedules, possible resistance to leaving the home, the nature of the medical office environment, and wait time. Then will come the potential "intrusion" of the doctor, and your loved one's response. At this point it is not reasonable or necessary for the person with Alzheimer's to accompany the holder of a power of attorney (POA) to the accountant or attorney. I suggest not bringing the matter to attention. If there are papers to be signed, the affected loved one is more likely to be agreeable in familiar surroundings. Again, when the person with dementia is in 24/7 care, the medical concerns are addressed daily at the facility unless there is a change requiring outside intervention. Socially, most friendships with the person with Alzheimer's have ceased or changed dramatically as most folks outside (or inside) the families have begun to shy away and are discomforted by of the affected person's variable behavior and cognitive decline. Maintaining social relationships is imperative for the spouse of the person with Alzheimer's disease. If the family member with Alzheimer's lives with a spouse or family, this becomes very difficult, as there *must* be a responsible older teen or adult in the home at all times with the person with Alzheimer's. When the person is placed in a full care situation this becomes easier, but brings other concerns: guilt may arise because you, the caregiver, are free to come and go as you please, but your loved one is in a facility with "no outs."

4. **Development of end plan:** This has been changed from the earlier phases' "development of a long range action plan." No longer are we thinking and planning strategies for the continuing care of our affected loved one. Our loved one is nearing the time of their death, and our plans must include shorter range determinations. Complete care for emotional, social and functional living is required for loved ones with Alzheimer's as they slip into their *own world* and do not visibly recognize family members. Decisions must be made regarding quality and longevity of life. This can be a very difficult period for families. Complicating questions may include:

   o When do you decide to stop feeding your loved one?
   o What if the person with Alzheimer's develops another disease or disorder, or is injured and you must decide whether to treat it or not?
   o How much treatment do you provide?
   o What if the person with Alzheimer's stops accepting the food, liquids, or exercise that you provide?

People with Alzheimer's disease cannot look their loved ones in the eye and let them know they are not hungry or thirsty right now, or they are no longer going to accept nourishment at all—that at some level they are ready to move on. We must all be aware of the cues given and accept the inevitable. These situations do happen, and the family will decide the course of action (there may be wishes expressed in a living will that must be considered). My experience is that families will make decisions earlier on in the disease process, only to question themselves or each other when in the moment of decision.

5. **The challenge of change:** The focus during the moderate phase of the disease was on the changes on the social and cognitive losses of the loved one, the family's acceptance of those losses, and the family's reclamation of an altered system. Now the person with Alzheimer's loses most social graces and behavioral understanding and truly loses the sense of self. In a sense the worst is over for people in this phase of Alzheimer's disease because, moving through this phase, they no longer realize what they have lost. Vague familiarity remains with some family members, although names and the kind of relationship no longer matters to them. Early on the person with Alzheimer's may smile or appear to enjoy receiving visits, but as soon as the visitors are gone, they were never there!

The challenges for the family become letting go of any expectations that their loved one will regain a former level of awareness and cognitive ability; *electing* someone to make very difficult decisions in the upcoming time their loved one remains alive; and putting forward their best efforts at maintaining their strength and their conviction that the loved one's dignity has been worth the pain and suffering. This acceptance and knowledge may be their only sense of satisfaction throughout the entire disease continuum. Another challenge rests with the further inclusion of non-family members into their lives. This becomes more frequent as, for example, medical changes cause emergency room visits. Infections, sores, wounds, and changes in eyesight, hearing, and dental hygiene are common. When swallowing becomes more difficult for the person with Alzheimer's and changes in food consistency are warranted, or when the risk of falling is heightened, speech and physical therapists may be brought to assess and possibly initiate changes.

6. **Grief:** How long does grief last? This is not a trick question. The type of grief family members suffer with Alzheimer's is like no other type. There are other terminal diseases—for example, forms of cancer—that strike at the hearts of families, performing their deed slowly, with suffering and pain to all those involved. The dementias rob loved ones not only of their physical presence on their way to death but also of the time when most families want to share final moments with their loved one, providing dignity and allowing for the cherished goodbyes. With Alzheimer's, the person with the disease has said goodbye months and even years before passing; long before we, as family, are ready to. How do you say goodbye to someone with Alzheimer's

so they know and remember the moment? That *is* a deceptive question, because you cannot.

7. **Guilt:** Most families have offered their very best to help their loved one make the transition with the least amount of pain and emotional challenge, while attempting to keep the dignity and positive memories of their loved one. Questions about whether the *right* decisions were made, if the time was *right* to move their family member into the long-term facility, and whether the *right* medical decisions were made continue to envelop the family thinking. Help comes from outside support, from support groups, professionals, or others who have been through this terrible ordeal. There are standards of care involving comfort, medical and other professional treatment, and stability for a person with Alzheimer's disease, but the journey through this disease is personal. Each person afflicted with this disease passes through the phases with individual challenges and at their own pace. We as families, with our care and love, may prolong their *walk* but not detour or stop it. **Letting go of our illusion of control over Alzheimer's disease means letting go of any guilt we have regarding the disease.**

SUPPORTING CASES

The following cases present PATTERNS of signs and symptoms that are common to families with similar circumstances at this phase of the disease. Not all changes in the person with Alzheimer's can be fully attributed to the advancement of dementia. Previously existing problems caused by co-existing disease processes, environmental or social factors, or medicine reactions may cause or exacerbate the dementia symptoms.

I am presenting these cases from my practice (names and details have been changed) to help give you a sense of the scope of how the disease presents itself, and the effects it can have on family systems. Your family situation will differ from the presented cases in various ways. **At the end of each case** *presentation and discussion, you'll find space where you can consider how your family situation is like or not like that case.*

As you read the cases, consider the following action items, as a starting point to develop a plan for how you will move through the transitions that the disease brings about. You'll find space **at the end of this Supporting Cases section** *where you can plan your responses for these action points.*

- **What concrete plans must be put into motion at this time?**
- **Who will be in charge of implementing the plans?**
- **Do you require an action plan for medical, psychiatric, or legal assistance?**

- What professionals or organizations will need to be contacted?
- Who will be the "Point Person" in charge of coordinating care needs with professionals and handling the unforeseen and acute situations that will arise?
- What support networks need to be established to provide care and education for family members?

CASE 1 Advanced Phase

This case represents the continuation of Case 4, Early and Moderate Phases.

Sam: Husband with Alzheimer's   Lucille: Wife
Caitlyn: Adult daughter   Janae: Adult daughter

It is eight months since the last noted changes in this case, and Sam and Lucille continue to live in their home. Since their daughter Janae made an unexpected visit and discovered the extent of her father's decline, the daughters have been increasingly involved with financial support and increased visiting. Lucille continued to dismiss the notion that Sam required full-time care until the last episode that ended with Sam in the emergency room at the local hospital. Sam has not been able to "help" Lucille around the house but requires her to be within listening or sight distance. He becomes disoriented moving from one room to the next and walks aimlessly, often talking to himself. Lucille has resisted in-home care except for someone to come and clean two times a month. Sam is incontinent during the night and wears Depends to bed. Lucille must wait for Sam to fall asleep because he insists on wanting to be sure the house is safe and his sleep habits have changed dramatically. He naps during the day, awakens about four in the morning, and wanders around the house. Both daughters have stayed for several days at a time, helping their mother care for their father and taking care for their father and take care of other necessary responsibilities. Food shopping and other local errands have been taken on by Lucille's close friend Fran.

Sam does not recognize his grandchildren any longer because of the infrequency of their visits. Fortunately, both of Sam's daughters have spent much time explaining to their children the changes that are occurring with Sam. When they visit, they bring pictures they drew and show Sam photos of them with him and Lucille. To date, he has been patient for short periods, but he loses interest quickly and says to Lucille, "What nice boys and girls these children are." During the last visit that included the grandchildren, Sam became incontinent and it turned out to be an embarrassing situation. Sam spends time looking at magazines with no memory of what he has looked at. There have been several visits to the medical doctor, and Sam has been diagnosed with high blood pressure but otherwise remains medically healthy.

Last week Lucille scheduled a hair appointment in the afternoon, a time that Sam typically naps for a few hours. Lucille's friend Fran came over to sit with Sam while he slept and care for his needs if Lucille was not yet home when he woke up. Sam has recognized Fran during her visits and was polite, with minimal interaction. On this occasion, Sam awakened prior to Lucille's return and wandered into the family room to find Fran sitting on the sofa. She casually said hello. Sam immediately left the room and began searching for Lucille, calling out her name. When Fran followed him into the kitchen, Sam turned and started to yell at her to get out of his house and bring Lucille back. Fran tried to soothe Sam, but he only became increasingly agitated. Suddenly he reached for a large cutlery knife and pointed it at Fran. She tried to talk to him but he was not able to listen. He moved toward her, and she left the room and called 911. Lucille came back to their home greeted by police and emergency medical technicians.

Sam was able to identify the police uniforms, and the police had knowledge of how to work with someone who has dementia. Sam gave up his knife and the police watched him until Lucille arrived. He was sobbing when she walked into the kitchen. Sam was taken to the emergency room at the local hospital. He could not recall the details of the event. He was calmed with medication and Lucille was able to take him home. The police report would be sent through the proper channels and hopefully Sam would not receive time in jail. Fran, who was very sympathetic, told Lucille that she would no longer be spending time with Sam unless Lucille was present.

Changes noted in the person with dementia and the family:

In Sam:
- Requires that his spouse be within sight or listening distance
- Exhibits high level of disorientation and confusion even while in their home
- Has delusions with potential for violence
- Is incontinent during the night
- Sleep patterns changed; spouse must be with him when he falls asleep

For the family:
- Taking Sam shopping is an unpredictable experience
- Sam does not recognize the children as his grandchildren
- Spouse provides high level of support and direct care
- Extended family financially is supportive, but offers minimal hands-on care
- Grandchildren involved with their grandfather with short visits, providing photos and drawings

Effects and Interventions

• This is a case that has progressed to the point of danger for those involved with the daily situation. It appears on the surface that the family has made many of the correct moves with providing Sam a loving and safe environment. He has someone present, his basic needs are provided, he receives medical attention and family visits. The tragedy here is that, regardless of how well the family had planned and lived their daily routine to maximize Sam's ability to stay at home, there comes a time when the critical changes caused by the disease create an unpredictable situation with a potential for danger. The loss for those with Alzheimer's disease can be slow; it can be difficult to discern the sometimes subtle decline. In this phase of the disease, delusions are more apparent, sometimes pronounced, and can affect even simple routines. Because they are combined with increased emotional discharge and confusion, all involved must develop an ability to live more in the moment. This situation especially addresses the unpredictability of those with this disease. Sam *normally* naps during the time Lucille had her appointment, and so she thought it was safe to leave for a few hours. To repeat: **there is no normal at this phase of the disease.**

• Lucille has been trying to take on the majority of the responsibility for care of Sam. She receives limited assistance from her daughters and from Fran, but she is primary caregiver—which, on most days, has required 24/7 care. This level of commitment has increased Sam's dependence on her, which also increases her drive to provide more care! Sam is going to become more dependent as the disease progresses, provided he remains cognizant of who Lucille is and of their relationship. By keeping Sam in the home to this point and providing the level of care she has until now, Lucille has created a higher degree of difficulty for the imminent transition that must take place. Lucille's level of care until now has a double edge. She has spent all the time she could with her husband, giving the best care possible and, at the same time, has possibly ignored the changes in Sam that created the dangerous situation. Hindsight is 20/20. The question of when to move a person with Alzheimer's disease to a more structured environment is different for each family situation, and is always difficult.

• The legal system is now involved. This situation could go in several possible directions. There will be a decision by the local jurisdiction of whether to pursue charges against Sam. If charges are pursued, the outcomes may include jail time, probation, or dismissal with or without conditions. Whatever course the legal decision follows, the effect on Sam and the family could be enormous, including increased confusion, fear, and anger from Sam and difficult adjustments with the family. A psychological evaluation will most assuredly be completed, and the outcome could determine the legal course followed by the authorities. The primary concern of the evaluation is to determine Sam's competency and his ability to show that he is capable of monitoring his daily life. This includes Sam's and others' safety and his decision-making and executive functioning skills. The family has serious decisions to make. The decisions could be determined by the course of actions set forth by any legal judgment, but the family would be wise to initiate their own timetable for change. Sam is not safe to remain in the environment he is in with the level of care he receives. It is obvious that he cannot be trusted to maintain clear thinking. He is delusional and capable of harm. Lucille must move forward to have Sam in a safer environment with full-time professional care. The burden of care must shift to people trained to work with this phase of the disease and for Lucille to learn a secondary care-giving role. There remain a number of ways for to continue her care on a personal, loving level without the responsibilities she had taken on previously.

In what ways is the above case different from or similar to your family situation?

_____

_____

_____

_____

_____

_____

CASE 2 Advanced Phase

This case represents the continuation of Case 5, Moderate Phase.

Sophia: Alzheimer's disease   Sol: Husband
Allan: Oldest son   Logan: Youngest son
Wendy: Daughter   Tyquan: Grandchild

It has been eight months since we last visited with Sol and Sophia, and they continue to live in their assisted living apartment. Sophia has continued to decline cognitively and behaviorally. Sol spends all of his day caring for her as she is prone to sudden mood changes, especially in social situations. She is active, moving items around the apartment daily, and then complaining about how the place looks. She rants at Sol, accusing him of having another woman and even shoving him a few times. Her sleep schedule has changed and she is awake for several hours each night. Sophia has refused to see the medical doctor for any concerns, and when she fell last week and refused to go to the emergency room; it was fortunate there was no serious problem. The children are aware of the situation but are attempting to assist from "away." Since the couple had already lost most of their close friends, Sol really gets no relief from the daily grind.

Last evening following dinner, Sol and Sophia were taking their nightly walk on the path surrounding the assisted living center when they met another couple walking in the opposite direction. Being polite, Sol said good evening; Sophia exploded in anger. She yelled at the woman to "stay away from my husband," calling her names and threatening to cause physical harm. At one point, Sophia raised her fist and verbally threatened to hit her right at that moment. Sol was able to redirect her and remove her from the situation, but Sophia was angry and accusatory all evening, not going into her bed until three AM. The next morning Sol called her family medical doctor and they spoke at length about the options for care. Sol thought he was ready to "pass the baton as primary caregiver."

As Sol saw it, the danger level of Sophia potentially doing harm to herself or another was escalating. Sol believed that he could no longer provide a safe environment in their current living situation. Following his conversation with the medical doctor, in which they explored several options, Sol called each of his children explaining the current situation and the choices for the upcoming decisions that were necessary to pursue. These decisions included a more restrictive living arrangement for Sophia and possible legal and financial considerations that could potentially affect all the children. Sol knows that this could be the final move for Sophia and has not approached his wife regarding his decision. He also knows that for the first time in sixty-plus years they will be separated.

Changes noted in the person with dementia and the family:

In Sophia:
- Higher levels of confusion in social situations
- Aggressive behavior toward her husband
- Sleep cycle has changed
- Social isolation has increased; loss of friends and daily contact outside of their apartment

- Unpredictable mood swings with delusional accusations and threats
- Dramatic need for increased personal care from her husband
- Refusal to seek medical attention
- Loss of ability to use and know the purpose of common objects

In the family:
- Family contact from afar, no daily support
- Husband recognizes the decline of his wife and necessity of a more restricted safe environment
- Husband has kept clear, open communication with his daughters regarding the changing events

Effects and Interventions

- Sophia's general awareness of everyday life has been altered. In the earlier phase, she expressed general insight into most situations as they arose, and with help from Sol shifted to feeling safe and able to conform. At this point, her level of confusion has risen to hinder any productive functioning. She moves furniture around the apartment without apparent purpose, loses her way in the hallway, and has become a danger to herself and others. Sophia has gone from dialing wrong numbers to not knowing how to use the telephone and other mechanical and electrical appliances. It has become highly unsafe to leave her alone for any length of time. It appears that her ability to communicate basic needs remains, and that with a fixed routine she is more able to perform primary tasks, although any alteration or disruption will cause confusion and consequential reactions.

• There is a new level of isolation for Sophia and Sol. They have lost their local friends and family has chosen distance care. Sophia is no longer able to leave the apartment without Sol, which binds them together full time. Sol's only known respite is when Sophia sleeps, and there appears to be no pattern to this time. The outcome for a situation where the spouse is the sole caregiver at this phase of the disease has un-welcome, predictable conclusions. With Sophia's changeable moods, dependency, and growing aggressiveness, Sol's level of tolerance will decrease. This could lead to reduced care, negligence, or potential spousal violence. Additionally, the likelihood that Sol will suffer emotional and physical fatigue is high. As the sole provider of care, any change in his well-being will have dire effects on Sophia's health.

• Sophia's level of distrust and paranoia has grown from the vague accusatory response to the delusional point of threat-ening to act upon her distortions without regard to the ef-fect her behaviors have herself or others. These symptoms are often treated medically, with agents that help to reduce the level of agitation and delusional activity. These medicines work in conjunction with behavioral and environmental cues that calm the person with Alzheimer's. The term "sun-down-ing" describes a situation when a person with Alzheimer's disease begins to show an increase in non-specific agitation, panic, and confusion. This commonly occurs in the mid-dle to late afternoon and has been associated with fatigue, late-day changes in lighting and shadows caused by the ap-proach of dusk, and possibly medication routine. Without medical intervention, Sophia's volatile behavior will increase and she becomes a risk for secondary problems, accidental self-harm, wandering and getting lost and more frightening delusions.

• Sophia has not been seen or evaluated by a medical or behavioral health professional for too long a period of time. There is high probability that what we are witnessing is Alzheimer's dementia, but without a medical and mental health diagnosis, we may be missing symptoms of other conditions. A parallel question might be, "What is the state of Sol's health?" Is he medically and psychologically capable of providing care for Sophia at this phase of the disease?

• Concern with not consulting professionals prior to this time includes the fact that Sophia was not understanding the changes taking place earlier in the disease process that could have eased this transition and allowed her more rewarding relationships with family and friends. Sol, with more information, might have altered future planning and arranged for a different housing arrangement earlier in the disease (with or near family; easier living arrangements for Sophia to manipulate and put advanced directives into place), and Sophia could have been an active participant in her life plan. Additionally, we do not know whether there have been legal steps taken to ensure the best care and management of their resources.

• Sophia has lost contact with all others except Sol. When shown photos of her grandchildren, she cannot identify them as such. She recognizes photos of her children but cannot name them or define their relationship to herself. If there was visitation by the family, younger children would want to have a "show and tell" with Grandma, but it is doubtful Grandma could engage. If she asked, "Who are these cute children?" family members who have not been actively involved and remained distant could be overwhelmed and children frightened. Attempting to provide any care-giving without easing into the *new relationship* would probably be rejected and met with fear by Sophia. Sol must recognize that he could lose some, if not all, of his family support with a decision to move Sophia to a more structured setting. A suggestion to help alleviate the possible resistance would be to have a professional knowledgeable with Alzheimer's facilitate the family discussion.

• The decision for a change in living arrangement requires Sol to bring in the grown children and develop a plan of action. This must be an on-site meeting. It is possible that one or more of the children may opt to remain at a distance for the remainder of their mom's life. Nevertheless, a meeting is needed to bring the family up to date and make necessary decisions. Sophia will undoubtedly resist *any change* proposed by Sol or anyone else. Any transition of living space for a person with dementia is difficult because of how hard it is to develop new routines in a new environment, with new people. Levels of confusion can increase, and some people do not recover earlier levels of functioning. Sophia may react with aggression, tears, and certainly fear about the changes. This will be extremely difficult for Sol, as he must listen to her teary pleadings, wrestle with any guilt at his decision, and learn to live life with dramatic changes. He most likely will live by himself and, having much more free time not caring for Sophia, he may face pronounced depression.

In what ways is the above case different from or similar to your family situation?

_____

_____

_____

_____

CASE 3 Advanced Phase

Gustav: Grandfather with Alzheimer's   Ged: Adult son
Mariola: Daughter-in-law
Stockton & Lloyd: Grandchildren (ages 9 & 6)

Gustav lives with his son, Ged, and his family. Daily in-home care is available while the boys are in school and both parents are working. Mariola is a nurse at the local hospital and Ged is an accountant. Gustav is highly disorganized in his behavior. In the morning, clothes are laid out on his bed and he requires assistance with each article of clothing. While he continues to feed himself, he sometimes gets confused with too much food and three utensils. Stockton and Lloyd, the two young grand-children, attempt to engage Gustav with books and games, but he becomes disinterested and will fall asleep while they read with him. At night, Ged will often be awakened by Gustav rum-maging in one of the closets or in the basement. He states that he is looking for his equipment to get ready for work. Early one morning about three weeks ago while Ged was redirect-ing his father back to his room, Gustav suddenly turned and shoved Ged against the wall. Ged did not tell anyone. Similar instances have occurred on two other occasions.

Two nights ago while Gustav and the grandchildren were watching television and Ged was still at work, Gustav soiled and wet his pants. The boys were scared and ran to their mother, who had to come and help Gustav clean up. Mariola was angry and raised her voice to Gustav, at which time he pushed her out of the way to get by. Later that night a fierce argument took place between Ged and Mariola. There were no conclusions about what, if any, changes were to occur in the household. Over the following two weeks, Stockton and Lloyd spent more time in their rooms following dinner. Mariola rarely spoke to Gustav, and Ged spent more time with his father administering direct care. Gustav became visibly more agitated. He paced more, slept and talked less, and refused to get out of his night clothes and get dressed on several mornings. There were several more incidences of Gustav soiling his pants while the care aide was in the home. Ged and Mariola are functional but the situation remains very tense.

Ged took his father to meet with their family physician and explain the changes that were taking place. Gustav presented fairly well, without incident, and stated that he felt okay, had no pain, and enjoyed living with his son and family. The doctor proceeded to ask Gustav several orientation questions and he failed to correctly identify the date, year, and president. He was vague in his ability to locate himself ("This is Arizona, isn't it"?). The doctor prescribed new medication for the increased behavioral concerns and suggested that it is time for Ged to consider moving his dad to a more restricted environment. Ged relayed this information to Mariola who said she knew of several facilities in the area that Ged could consider. Ged said that he wanted to give the newly prescribed medicine a chance. This infuriated Mariola and she threatened to take their children to go live with her mother until Gustav was out of their home.

Changes noted in the person with dementia and the family:

In Gustav:
- Becoming incontinent of urine and feces
- Having minimal interaction with the grandchildren

- Having difficulty using eating utensils appropriately; becoming more confused with daily routine
- Requires full assistance with dressing daily
- Exhibits increased agitation and intermittent aggression towards the adults in the family

In the family:
- The grandchildren have become frightened of their grandfather and spend increased time in their rooms.
- The grandchildren have been part of the care, attempting to occupy Gustav's time through games and reading. This tactic is no longer working.
- At present they have in-home care during the day, but when "sun-downing" occurs and behaviors have a tendency to escalate, the burden of care falls on the family.
- With the latest decline in Gustav's daily functioning, the family is under increasingly difficult stress.
- Ged feels a great loyalty to keep his father in the home.
- The dynamics of home life have changed to the point of causing a rift in the marriage between the son and his wife.

Effects and Interventions

- Gustav is highly confused and cannot follow through on any serial tasks without another's assistance (dressing, eating, bowel and urinary functions). This is not uncommon as this phase of the disease progresses. Safely performing daily functions is the integral component of independent living, and it appears Gustav has lost that ability. Even simple tasks require some degree of reasoning and judgment. For example, when I lift a fork to my mouth, it is because there is food on it. I know when to lift it to my lips and when to take it away. I know to use my fork and not my knife. I know to chew and swallow my food before getting another mouthful. Gustav's ability to perform even these simple tasks is fading and, at this point, the family carries the burden to assist. They are not trained to offer that assistance and, considering the aggression already shown, it is not a safe responsibility for them to have.

• Safety is the other major concern. Gustav has been violent for at least a month. It appears that he can be indiscriminate and unpredictable. The higher the level of confusion, the greater the risk for further violence. Even though the grandchildren are spending less time with Gustav, they do have meals and other common times together, and Gustav is wandering with a disrupted sleep cycle. The concern for safety is not only relegated to the other family members. Gustav may take to wandering outdoors and get lost. It is doubtful that he is spatially oriented to more than just the household, considering that this is his family's home and he moved here earlier during the disease process. Additionally, as Gustav becomes increasingly frail or is prescribed more medication that causes sleepiness, his fall risk increases.

• The grandchildren have "lost" their grandfather. They are young and would clearly not understand the changes they observe in him. He had been less responsive and interactive, and he frightened them when he became incontinent. The grandkids have withdrawn to their rooms. It is essential that both parents begin to address these concerns with their

160

children. Their ability to continue providing some form of "assistance" to Grandpa will help to ease their fear and sense of displacement. Sitting with Grandpa, showing him old photos, reading a story, or coloring pictures to hang in his room could keep them invested. Unfortunately, at this time, the level of stress occurring between the adults in the home may preclude the attention they require.

• Ged and Mariola are struggling. Even with daily full-time help for Gustav, there is tension. Weekends and evenings are focused around his safety and care. Restful sleep for Ged is disrupted. Now, with Gustav's increased incontinence, Ged is the primary hygiene caregiver, and a role-reversal has occurred. With Ged spending more time tending to the needs of his father, Mariola has increasingly begun to feel the strain: less time with Ged and less time as a family foursome. Gustav recently pushed Mariola out of the way when her frustration came through. With Ged so involved with the care for his father, to whom can Mariola freely speak her mounting frustrations? This issue requires immediate attention. At the end of the case presentation, Mariola throws down the gauntlet! If something is not done to move Gustav from their home, she and the boys will go to live with her mother. To get to that point in the situation, it appears that much has not been said between Ged and Mariola to work this through.

• Ged took his father to a medical doctor and it appears that, although Gustav presented calmly, he was disoriented and confused. He was prescribed medication to reduce the behavioral concerns. Hopefully, the medication would help in this respect, but not without the potential for side effects that could leave Gustav more fatigued and unsteady—which presents new concerns. Additionally, there are the cognitive symptoms that cannot be addressed by the medications, and these will continue to erode Gustav's basic ability to understand information from the environment and express himself clearly to have his needs met. **The family does not have the training or perseverance to meet these oncoming expanding demands.** It is time for Ged to admit that he has done all he can for his father in the present environment and more professional full-time care is warranted. Ged would do well to consult with a psychologist or social worker and join a support group familiar with the struggles family members have during such times. A trained professional can also help him continue a healthy grieving for his personal loss while attending to the needs of his wife and children. There are placement issues regarding Gustav's relocation which involve financial questions and legal concerns to be calculated.

In what ways is the above case different from or similar to your family situation?

_____

_____

_____

_____

_____

_____

CASE 4 Advanced Phase

Fannie: Grandmother with Alzheimer's   Eunice: Daughter
Rhoda: Daughter   Carol: Daughter
Carlos: Grandson (age 19)

Fannie has been in the skilled nursing home for the past two and a half years. She suffers from Alzheimer's disease and has over the past several months lost six pounds, mainly because she doesn't remember how to use eating utensils. Her family is very attentive, and they come daily for two meals a day to assist with feeding her. When they help, Fannie eats better. She is slow, has some difficulty with swallowing, and her mouth must be cleaned following the meal to extract any food that remain so that she will not choke. Fannie, through facial expressions, *appears* to recognize her daughters, Eunice and Rhoda, most of the time. They live nearby and share responsibility for her care. Thinking they were smart and could help each other when these days finally arrived, they share power of attorney responsibilities. Carol, the third daughter, lives in San Diego and speaks to her siblings several times a week.

Prior to Fannie's admission to the skilled nursing facility (SNF), she was living with Eunice and her family. The grandchildren, ranging in age from 13 through 21, would tend to and spend much free time with Fannie and showed great love. When Fannie entered the SNF, they were part of the *team* that assisted with care and kept their grandmother occupied and focused. They decorated her room with photos and read to her whenever they visited. That continues to this day, although Fannie usually falls asleep and does not seem to understand their discussions. The SNF has daily programming for the residents, but Fannie rarely actively participates. She smiles when people come and play music; she will handle soft objects when they are put in her hand, but she does not interact with the other residents. Intermittently, she will speak words out of context without meaning directed to a situation. If asked a simple question such as "Are you thirsty?" Fannie may nod her head in response, although when someone puts a cup to her lips she will turn her head away from the cup.

Last week Carol came for the weekend and spent a good part of both days with her mother. Before she left, the family had a discussion about Mom and her situation. Carol was adamant that the family should not be *force feeding* their mother. By her own admission, Carol believed that her mother did not seem to recognize her. She was visibly upset and shaken by the loss of verbal communication and her mother's lack of independent ability for self-care. Eunice and Rhoda were taken aback and an angry exchange ensued. How could Carol come in for one long weekend and make a judgment that would probably end their mother's life? How could they call what Mom was going through life, Carol countered? There was little doubt that if the assisted feeding were to end, Fannie would pass. Carol insisted that their mother, and grandmother, would not want to live with people feeding her, dressing her, and cleaning her, and that the family was more interested in *their need* to care for Fannie than in her dignity. Her sisters called Carol insensitive and not caring for their mother, saying that if she loved her as they did, she would be there more often and assist as they were. Then she would understand what and why they were providing the way they were.

The oldest grandchild, Carlos, who was mostly silent during these exchanges, spoke up, asking, "Will we ever be ready to say goodbye to Grandma?"

Changes noted in the person with dementia and the family:

In Fannie:
- Cannot self-feed; requires assistance for all nutritional intake
- Requires assistance for all ADL's
- Appears to exhibit only intermittent facial recognition of some family members
- Words are sparse; communication is not reliable
- Does not interact with other residents or staff during activities
- Appears to experience some satisfaction from environmental stimulation (music, handling objects)

In the family:
- Two of Fannie's daughters and some grandchildren remain active with her daily care
- The third daughter disagrees with feeding their mom to keep her alive
- The oldest grandchild expresses concern regarding how the family is grieving their situation

Effects and Interventions

- Fannie retains her ability to perform minor tasks on a daily basis. Most tasks require several steps, and while she cannot perform the beginning, middle, and end of most given tasks, she can be cued and assisted to perform partial completion.

For example, Fannie can chew her food but may not be able to use the proper utensil, find her mouth, or move the utensil to get more food following a bite. She may be able to use the toilet but must be placed upon it or reminded that she may have to go. She will not be able to call out and request a drink when she is thirsty but *knows* when she is! When Eunice and Rhoda come to visit, she will not be able to call them by name but able to give non-verbal facial recognition of their presence. We could tempt ourselves and say that Fannie has *forgotten* much of what she has learned over her lifetime, but I would challenge that notion and suggest rather that she remembers differently or partially. **Memory is not an on/off switch but a dimmer dial that fades over time.** The work of the family, significant others, and aides who continue to be part of Fannie's life is to identify what remains of her *self-identity*, find ways to make connections and keep her functioning, and know when she is ready only for basic comfort care.

• Eunice and Rhoda, the two daughters who live locally, have been dedicated to maintaining the care and dignity of their mother over an extended period during the progress of the disease. As is common, the person with Alzheimer's will exhibit temporary periods of what seem to be clarity in communication and behavior, which affords the family glimpses of her former self. This is a double-edged sword for the caregivers. Recognizing and accepting the steady and sometimes very subtle changes in the person with dementia, even at this phase, can be difficult for anyone losing a loved one. Carol, the daughter who lives a distance away from her mom and has not seen her for an extended period, observes the dramatic changes that have occurred. Her perspective contradicts that of her siblings and challenges them to review their position. This is a common family dynamic with families who have varying levels of interaction with the affected loved one. This situation may potentially have a scarring effect on the future relationship of the siblings with accusations of lack of caring and sensitivity on one side and of selfish reasons for keeping Mom alive on the other. If Carol is proposing a different action plan at this time and decides to become more actively involved, there may be a necessity for professional intervention to mediate and discuss the options. It is important to note that families can avoid potential stressful and challenging conversations by researching *advanced directives* options which are generally completed while a loved can participate in their advanced planning.

• We have not heard what the professionals in this case have to offer regarding the level of care for Fannie. Should the SNF staff and family maintain the same care regime, or begin to look at a path primarily promoting comfort care? Considering the inclusion of Carol into the mix of opinions, it would be proper and informative to have a conference with the medical and/or behavioral health specialist and representatives of the daily care staff to discuss a plan. At this point, Fannie would not be able to contribute meaningful information to the plan. It is not until faced with a situation of this sort that family members recognize the enormous impact of their decisions. Another factor to consider is that there has not been any mention of co-existing conditions that could affect the plan. Another medical condition that affects the person with Alzheimer's ability to eat or breathe or level of pain would be a factor in devising the continuing plan. It would be advantageous for the family to engage hospice for further assistance with care.

• Another set of voices to be heard from are the grandchildren. Carlos' prophetic declaration stated at the end of the case presentation is a telling indication that he, at least, is emotionally attached to the outcome of this situation and Grandma's well-being. Is he representative of the other grandchildren or speaking only for himself? Indications from the case suggest that if the other grandchildren are involved with care, even peripherally, they would want to have their voices heard in the decision-making process, if for nothing else than to express their feelings and concerns. It can be easy for the older adults in the family to proclaim that they have the right to make the decisions regarding their parent(s). Keeping communication open with all family members is important.

In what ways is the above case example different from or similar to your family situation?

_____

_____

_____

_____

_____

_____

CASE 5 Advanced Phase

Fernando: Husband with Alzheimer's   Carla: Wife
Rainee: Daughter   Joe: Son-in-law
grandchildren: ages 5 & 7)
Sylvia: Resident at nursing facility

Fernando had recently been relocated to one of the local skilled nursing facilities. He had been living with Carla, his wife, at their home for several years with in-home assistance. Their daughter and her family lived nearby and were regular visitors to their home. Yesterday, when Carla and two of her grandchildren went to visit at the skilled nursing facility, Fernando was holding hands with another female resident, Sylvia. They walked over to where Fernando and Sylvia were sitting. The grandchildren went to hug Fernando; he was polite and then asked who they were. The young children thought he was kidding and laughed. They said, "You know us, Grandpa, stop fooling around." Fernando did not respond. Carla said hello and Fernando introduced his "wife," Sylvia. Sylvia smiled and said nothing, as she obviously had dementia also. Carla started crying and left with the two children. Seeing her cry, the children also began to cry, although they were not sure why.

Carla went back to her daughter Rainee's home and told her and Joe, her husband, what had happened. Rainee was irate. She wanted to call the nursing facility immediately and speak to the administrator; she was ready to move her dad to another care facility. To her, this meant that the staff was not paying attention to the residents, and this was morally wrong. Joe was not as quick to respond and thought it would be a good idea to visit the next day to sort out the situation. Carla agreed, and decided to visit the next day without the grand-children before they spoke to anyone.

The next day the three adults revisited the care facility, and there were Fernando and Sylvia, sitting together watching television. Fernando had his arm over the back of the sofa where Sylvia sat next to him. They approached; Rainee said, "Hello, Father." Fernando said hello and introduced Sylvia, although not as his wife. Fernando also said hello to Carla and Joe. Carla asked if they could go to speak somewhere without Sylvia and he reluctantly agreed. He bent over, attempted to kiss Sylvia, and told her he would be back soon. After a half hour visit, the family went to the charge nurse to discuss the incident. The nurse listened and acknowledged that they do spend much time together during the day. Rainee became furious and started shouting at the nurse, demanding to speak with the administrator. She could not imagine that the staff was allowing "sexualized behavior" in the facility. Carla was in tears, and Joe was attempting to calm the situation.

They did have the opportunity to speak to the administrator with the nurse present. The administrator attempted to calm the family by explaining some identifying features of advanced phase dementia, with assurances that the residents were not having inappropriate physical relations. He did agree that holding hands and kissing were beyond appropriate and safe boundaries for the residents. Additionally, he gave the family pamphlets with information about Alzheimer's disease and suggested that they become involved in local support groups.

He strongly encouraged continued visitation by all members of the family.

Changes noted in the person with dementia and the family:

In Fernando:
- Has established a delusion of marriage with another resident at the skilled nursing facility
- Exhibits vague recognition of family members who came to visit
- Shows a high level of confusion and disorientation, possibly exacerbated by the recent move to the SNF

In the family:
- Adult family members are reacting to Fernando's "marital" relationship with another resident at the facility
- Grandchildren are active in the life of their grandfather; following the visit to the SNF, when Grandpa did not know them, and the reaction by Grandma, they may feel confused and possibly be left out of future family visits.

Effects and Interventions

- At this phase of the disease, Fernando has moderate to severe difficulty with general orientation and will have difficulty distinguishing familiar from unfamiliar persons, with limited recognition of familiar items or places. There is loss of recognition of other people—spouses, children, or other significant people in their lives. Hence the difficulty Fernando has in recognizing his grandchildren, his wife, and their significance to his life. With memory loss and distortion, Fernando could easily mistake another woman for his wife, given the daily living arrangement in the skilled nursing facility and the limited time he now spends with his real wife. No one could see this particular situation coming, but if one thinks about the level of distortion and confusion Fernando is now experiencing, coupled with living with females, it becomes more palatable that a demented man who has lived with his wife for many years and is suddenly in a new environment could believe another woman was his wife. Initially Carla is very angry; she is hurt and harshly confronts her loss. With her current level of understanding about Alzheimer's disease, her response appears appropriate. It is important to remember that **thinking logically and expecting a person with advanced dementia to think and act logically is illogical!**

• Recall is poor and recent memories are easily forgotten especially without daily reinforcement. People in this phase of the disease will often make comments regarding not being in their home (they may not recognize whether they are). Using life-story reminders can ease the agitation of people with Alzheimer's—personalizing their room with decorations that have individual significance, with reminders of who they were in their relationships and their general personhood. This may be one way for the grandchildren to become actively involved in the care. Working on photo displays or drawings and writing short notes can help the children feel included.

• It appears from this limited case that Fernando continues to retain global social skills. Even with the *wrong* woman he exhibits the *correct* social graces. We are not sure whether Fernando has forgotten who his grandchildren are, or whether he even comprehends the concept of grandchildren. We do know he understands what *wife* means! Fernando appears to have purpose, but at this phase his insight, judgment, and ability to understand how his behavior affects others are highly questionable. This is an important point; it illustrates how memory, as mentioned before, is not like an on/off switch but a more complicated process encompassing all the senses. Fernando remembers how to apply the term *wife* but doesn't remember whom to apply it to! It is also important to remember that Fernando is still in a state of transition and requires time to attain maximum adjustment to the facility.

• Education about Alzheimer's disease and how it affects the person with Alzheimer's, and the family, is critical for safety and adaptation to the myriad cognitive and behavioral transformations. It is urgent for the family to get further involved with knowledge and care to increase their understanding of the nature of this disease: reading, support groups, visitation, and discussion with each other (including the grandchildren) and professionals. The care facility could encourage this by providing time to meet with the family, explaining why they administer care the way they do, referring them to outside support groups, assisting the family in adapting to the downward changes their loved one will experience, and keeping them apprised of any changes. The facility's willingness to work with the family in this situation, accepting their concerns and looking into altering their care program, creates a strong alliance with the family. Greater knowledge makes possible better and safer decisions for the person with Alzheimer's disease and the family. For example, how should the family respond if Fernando was unpredictable, exhibiting dangerous behavior by striking out or using profane language? Such behaviors may be induced by medications, the environment, time of day, or other possible reasons. The possibility of the young grandchildren witnessing the behaviors may be high. With proper preparation by the family through education and professional support in coordination with the facility, the potential of the grandchildren witnessing these situations can be minimized.

In what ways is the above case different from or similar to your family situation?

_____

_____

_____

_____

_____

_____

CREATING AN ACTION PLAN

Now that you have read the cases illustrating the challenges of this phase of Alzheimer's disease, you may fill in the spaces after the following action items. I hope this can serve as a starting point to develop a plan for how you will move through the transitions that the disease brings about.

What concrete plans must be put into motion at this time?

_____

_____

_____

_____

Who will be in charge of implementing the plans?

_____

_____

_____

_____

Do you require an action plan for medical, psychiatric, or legal assistance?

_____

_____

_____

What professionals or organizations will need to be contacted?

_____

_____

_____

_____

Who will be the "Point Person" in charge of coordinating care needs with professionals and handling the unforeseen and acute situations that will arise?

_____

_____

_____

_____

What support networks need to be established to provide care and education for family members?

_____

_____

_____

_____

Chapter 4

Dementia

Segment One:
Dementia and the Brain

The brain is a complex organ, performing millions of functions per second that enable us to think, move, feel, and maintain communication and interaction with the outside world. The brain is divided into two hemispheres and four lobes, which coordinate the systems and house the parts that promote and carry on our life's functions. The National Alzheimer's Association defines *dementia* as a pattern of erosion in the brain that reduces and prohibits the completion of the intended mission by destroying neurological pathways and killing the neurons, so that over time, even our most basic functions will be lost. The dementias represent a collection of disorders that describe losses in thinking, behavior, and functional areas. The onset of dementia symptoms may be temporary or permanent depending on the initial cause. With Alzheimer's disease, the symptoms are progressive and eventually will lead to death. The course of the disease varies according to a number of factors, and the effect on the family can be prolonged and overwhelming. **One hallmark early warning sign of dementia, specifically early phase Alzheimer's disease, is poor retention of new information, which leads to repetitive questions and frustrating forgetfulness.** It is important to understand the basic principles of memory and the parts of the brain associated with memory and memory loss.

How Does the Brain Store Information?

Our brains are made of nerve cells and many other cell types. These nerve cells, called neurons, are located primarily in the cerebral cortex, which is proportionally much larger in humans than in any other animals. This region is where cognitive functions, like thinking, learning, speaking, remembering, and making decisions, take place. Crucial brain parts include:

- Limbic System: This area links the brain stem with the higher reasoning elements of the cerebral cortex. It controls emotions and instinctive behavior. It is also where the sense of smell is located.
- Hippocampus: Important for learning and short-term memory, this is where short-term memories are converted into long-term memories for storage in other brain areas.
- Thalamus: Receives sensory and limbic information, processes it, and then sends it to the cerebral cortex.
- Hypothalamus: This structure, under the thalamus, monitors activities like body temperature and food intake. It issues instructions to correct any imbalances. It also controls the body's internal clock.

Newer techniques in medical technology give us vast amounts of knowledge as to how the different parts of the brain work together. A Magnetic Resonance Image (MRI) uses a magnetic tube that views the internal structures of the brain. It is a diagnostic tool that detects any abnormalities in the body such as bleeding, trauma or blockage in the arteries. Positron emission tomography (PET) measures blood flow and glucose metabolism throughout the brain, showing these functions as highlighted color. The tracers can track the activity of brain chemicals, like neurotransmitters such as dopamine and serotonin. Some of these neurotransmitters are altered with age, disease, and drug treatment.

Memory and Loss

Memory—an extremely complex cognitive process that involves different parts of the brain—reflects a person's abilities to draw on recent or remote information to which he or she has been exposed. Problems with memory may be manifested as forgetting names, dates, places, or whether appointments are kept. Instructions for a new or familiar game or work project will have to be repeated several times because the person cannot accurately remember the correct sequence of steps to complete the assignment. Memory impairment may be associated with poor attention, depression, delirium, medications, substance abuse, and a number of other medical and/or psychological issues. Memory lapses may be acute or chronic, may disappear, or may get worse. Memory loss may induce secondary problems and fears, or be used as an excuse for noncompliance or compensation!

In early adulthood, you begin to lose brain cells at a slow pace. Some neurons shrink especially larger ones in areas important to learning, memory, planning, and other complex mental activities. Because we have billions of neurons and myriad pathways available, the loss we incur is not detected at a younger age. Our bodies also start to make less of the chemicals that brain cells need to work. In addition, there are free radicals, a kind of molecule that reacts with other molecules and causes a lack of neural functioning. The older you are, the more these changes can affect your memory.

These changes affect memory in the aging brain including the way memories are accumulated, making it harder to recall stored information. Age-related memory which includes recent recall may be affected. For example, you may forget names of people you've met today or where you set your keys. These are normal changes.

"Think of the brain's hippocampus as the librarian and the rest of the brain as the vast library. With an ineffective librarian you will not be able to gain quick and complete access to all of the information that's stored in the brain," explains Dr. Michael Yassa. The real trouble, Dr. Yassa states, "is that our aging brains are unable to process new information because the pathways that make up the hippocampus become degraded over time. The brain's librarian never gets to catalog the new information correctly" (Yassa 2011).

The hippocampus and the prefrontal cortex are located in the temporal lobe of the brain. Damage to this area effects *episodic memory* which is involved with learning new information and remembering recent events. *Semantic memory* is involved with general knowledge and facts. This includes a person's ability to name and categorize objects (name a horse and put it in the "animal" category). The temporal lobe and possibly areas of the cortex are involved. *Working memory* presides over attention, concentration and short-term retention of needed information like phone numbers or grocery lists. Loss of this function could impair a person's ability to multi-task. The pre-frontal cortex is the primary area of the brain that is affected. Working memory can be affected by several cognitive disorders including Alzheimer's, Parkinson's, Huntington's and dementia with Lewy Bodies. *Procedural memory* enables us to learn skills that become automatic like skiing or riding a bike. The cerebellum is involved with procedural memory damage and is not affected by Alzheimer's disease.

With dementia, the degree of memory loss is a key determining ingredient for treatment and safety decisions. It is said that someone with Alzheimer's has memory loss. But what does that mean? As already stated, we all have some memory loss, caused by various internal or external circumstances. Depending on the initial cause, some memory loss can be reversed or slowed. But with the dementias, the memory loss is irreversible and eventually can spread to all facets of memory. There are many different types of memory. As Dr. John Zeisel notes in his book *I'm Still Here*, we have memories of sense, emotion, skill, body, and art. We even have what he considers hard-wired memories that may remain well into the disease process. The point is that *people continue to remember! The situation is not like a light with an on/off switch. The memory switch has a dimmer attached!* One particular problem with measuring memory accurately in people with Alzheimer's disease is that they may have other cognitive problems that inhibit or distort their ability to effectively communicate what they are experiencing. Therefore, it becomes imperative to *read* the facial or other nonverbal expressions of the person with Alzheimer's. This is also necessary to determine pain, anxiety, anger, or any other emotion or reaction.

Segment Two:
About the Dementias

Dementia has a Latin origin (actually two words) which translates as *away* and *mind*. It is defined as a deterioration of intellectual faculties, such as memory, concentration, and judgment, resulting from an organic disease or a disorder of the brain. It is sometimes accompanied by emotional disturbance and personality changes. Often the disease produces memory loss, visual and spatial distortions, loss of executive functions (insight, judgment, reasoning, organization, planning), mood deterioration, independent function loss, and voluntary motor/ behavior loss of control (Mace 1999). **Dementia does not mean crazy!**

Although dementia has always been somewhat common, it has become increasingly recognized in recent decades due to improvements in diagnostic techniques. In addition, people have longer life expectancies now, and thus are more likely to develop dementia as a function of older age. The diagnosis of dementia is intended to encompass the spectrum of severity, ranging from the mildest to the most severe phases of dementia. Dementia is diagnosed when there are cognitive or behavioral (neuropsychiatric) symptoms that:

- Interfere with the ability to function at work or at usual activities
- Represent a decline from previous levels of functioning and performing
- Are not explained by delirium or a major psychiatric disorder
- The cognitive or behavioral impairment involves a minimum of two of the following domains:
  o Impaired ability to acquire and remember new information
  o Impaired reasoning and handling of complex tasks, poor judgment
  o Impaired visual-spatial abilities
  o Impaired language functions
  o Change in personality, behavior, or comportment

Dementia is a generic term, and accordingly there are a number of different types.

Cortical Dementias

These dementias arise from a disorder affecting the cerebral cortex (the outer layers of the brain), which plays a critical role in thinking abilities like memory and language. People with cortical dementia typically show severe memory loss and aphasia (the inability to express and understand speech). These dementias are nonreversible and include:

Alzheimer's Dementia (60–80% of dementias):

Approximately 500,000 people under the age of 65 have Alzheimer's disease (AD) or some other dementia. Additionally, 5.4 million Americans 65 and older have AD Right now, someone in America develops AD every 69 seconds. By 2050, based on population and life expectancy, that frequency will be every 33 seconds. The estimates are that by mid-century as many as 11 to 16 million Americans over the age of 65 will have AD. Recent estimates predict 6% 65-74, 44% 75-84 and 46% aged 85 and older afflicted. On average, a person with Alzheimer's lives approximately four to eight years from the original diagnosis and some individuals as long as twenty years. Experts believe that barely half of the millions afflicted have actually been diagnosed, and from this group, only 20% have been treated in any clear therapeutic fashion. The National Institute on Aging estimates that direct and indirect annual costs for caring for individuals with AD are at least $200 billion in 2012. The annual cost for an AD patient at home from diagnosis to death is approximately $25,800 for community dwelling care. If a person cannot be cared for at home and must be cared for at a skilled nursing facility, the annual cost runs to approximately $70,000.

Alzheimer's disease disrupts each of the three processes that keep neurons healthy: communication, metabolism, and repair. This disruption causes certain nerve cells in the brain to stop working, lose connections with other nerve cells, and finally die. In addition to memory failure, the destruction of nerve cells causes personality changes, problems in carrying out daily activities, and other features of the disease. The brains of patients with AD have an abundance of two abnormal structures: **beta-amyloid plaques** and **neurofibrillary tangles.** This is especially true in areas of the brain that are most important to memory. Plaques are dense, mostly insoluble deposits of protein and cellular material outside and around the neurons. Tangles are insoluble twisted fibers that build up inside the nerve cell. A signature sign of Alzheimer's disease is the exaggerated buildup of tangles and plaques that develop in neurons and surrounding areas to cause the extensive damage and loss of cognitive function.

Alzheimer's disease results from multiple factors. Non-genetic factors, such as free radical damage linked with oxidative stress, disease-related brain inflammation, and damage associated with brain infarcts (dead tissues), are believed to play a role in the disease. More recent studies are strongly suggesting closer ties to heart disease, diabetes, obesity and poor eating habits, traumatic brain injury and lack of physical fitness.

Alzheimer's disease involves multiple cognitive deficits expressed through memory impairment and at least one of the following: Aphasia, apraxia, agnosia, and disturbance of executive functions. These declines will cause significant impairment in social or occupational functioning. As noted, loss of short-term memories is often the first symptom. Gradually, loss of thinking skills and other symptoms emerge, such as language difficulty, impaired judgment, mood changes, and the ability to carry out even the simplest tasks. A person diagnosed with symptoms of Alzheimer's that alter daily life prior to age 65 would be diagnosed with **younger onset Alzheimer's dementia**.

Younger Onset Alzheimer's Dementia
Approximately 5 percent of the people who develop Alzheimer's disease do so before the age of 65. This is generally known as Alzheimer's dementia with early onset. With roughly 5 million people, and growing, affected by Alzheimer's disease, at least 200,000 people have been diagnosed with the younger onset form of the disease. Younger onset has been known to develop as early as at 30 to 40 years of age, but it is more common to be diagnosed in the late 50s to early 60s. Younger onset Alzheimer's disease may run in families with a sibling and/or parent (first degree relatives) who also developed Alzheimer's at a younger age.

According to the National Institute on Aging, if a parent has the familial form of younger onset Alzheimer's disease, children have a 50 percent chance of developing the condition. This is called *Familial Alzheimer's Disease (FAD)*. In addition to lifestyle and environmental factors, there are generally three genes associated with this form of Alzheimer's, which makes the genetic potential much stronger in this form of the disease. Alzheimer's disease before the age of 65 would be more expected if you have a genetic mutation on the APP, PS1, or

PS2 genes. This is a different genetic marker than the APO-E (Apolipoprotein E) commonly associated with an increased risk of late onset Alzheimer's disease. This genetic disposition accounts for 1% of causality.

There is a perception that younger onset Alzheimer's disease does progress at a faster rate, but there is no hard data to support the claim. If one judges entry into a nursing facility as the determining factor for progress of the disease, then it could be that people suffering from early onset would seem to progress faster due to the impact on family members' daily costs and the complications for their more active lives. Additionally, it may take longer for the symptoms to be noticeable in healthier people. People who develop early onset may still have children at home and elderly parents who require care; they may work full time and feel overwhelmed with the complicating factors.

There are pros and cons for deciding to have younger family members participate in genetic testing for this form of Alzheimer's. Coping with the knowledge at 15 years old that you may develop an incurable disease when you get older would be a very difficult emotional burden to carry and would have dramatic implications for you and significant others in your future life.

Indicators of early onset Alzheimer's disease are similar to those of the late onset form. These symptoms include regularly losing items, difficulty in executing common tasks, forgetfulness, personality changes, confusion, poor judgment, challenges with basic communication and language, social withdrawal, and problems following simple directions (G. Smith 2011).

On November 3, 1906, Alois Alzheimer, M.D., co-presented a professional paper to the South West German Society of Alienists. This was the first examination describing a clinical case of dementia. The patient died in April 1906. Dr. Alzheimer examined the brain, and his discovery of plaques and neurofibrillary tangles led to his hypothesis that there was an organic cause for her condition. The paper, only three pages long in translation, describes symptoms that included disorientation, aphasia, auditory hallucinations, paranoia, unpredictable behavior, and pronounced psychosocial impairment. At the time, there was no attempt to consider any sort of social or environmental impairment. The patient's past life and institutional incarceration seem to have been ignored completely as a possible explanation of her mental state. Dr. Alzheimer's description of organic changes, atrophy, neurofibrillary tangles, and plaques linked to dementia was not a new discovery, yet it is his name that we link to dementia in most cases.

At the time, Dr. Emil Kraepelin was attempting to classify illness and disease as both organic and psychiatric. Dr. Kraepelin is now known for his pivotal work in the classification of schizophrenia. He was the one who incorporated the study by Dr. Alzheimer into his eighth edition (1910) textbook *Psychiatrie*. Dr. Kraepelin stressed the role of organic changes occurring in the brain in his theories of mental illness. He described "Alzheimer's disease" as both a distinctive disease that resulted from the action of a single cause and a distinct subcategory of senile dementia.

Dr. Alzheimer's collegial relationship with Dr. Kraepelin was certainly a major factor in having this newly classified disease named after him. Dr. Kraepelin was making a name for himself as the head of the large Munich academic institution. Honoring someone from the same department increased the prestige and influence of the institution.

Alois Alzheimer died at age 51 of tonsillitis, which had resulted in nephritis (severe inflammation of the kidneys). In his lifetime he published 19 papers on subjects as diverse as epilepsy, the classification of psychiatry, and general paresis (muscular weakness), as well as on dementia. He could have little idea that his name would become an internationally understood description of a disease suffered by millions of people.

Other (Non-Alzheimer's) Cortical Dementias

Vascular Dementia (Multi-Infarct Dementia) (10–20%):

This type of dementia is caused by the accumulated effect of repeated strokes in various areas of the brain. Symptoms often overlap with those of Alzheimer's, although memory loss is often milder and physical disability worse. Impending effects depend on the number of strokes and the location of the damage in the brain. The use of medications to treat the causative factors of the mini-strokes and other changing health factors could slow or quicken the dementia symptoms one would experience. In some cases, a stroke may be a triggering mechanism for the onset of Alzheimer's. Worsening of symptoms often occurs in a stepwise fashion as repeated strokes cause additional brain damage. (Mace 1999)

Fronto-temporal Dementia (FTD) (approximately 20%):

This type of dementia has symptoms similar to those of Alzheimer's. Behavior disturbances, such as disinhibition (behaving in socially unaccepted ways or making statements with little or no respect to consequences), withdrawal, or repetitive/compulsive behaviors outweigh memory impairment along with executive function loss. This function is generally impaired early in the disease. One widely accepted method of measuring executive functioning is requesting a person to draw a clock, noting the clock face with numbers and the clock hands pointing to a specific time. This activity measures losses to planning, organization, and achieving a complex series of activities. Memory impairment generally occurs at a later stage. FTD usually occurs in adults between the ages of 40 and 70. Other names for FTD are Pick's disease, progressive aphasia, semantic dementia, and frontal dementia of the non-Alzheimer's type. Approximately 40% of patients with FTD have family histories of a similar dementia syndrome. Other possible symptoms include inappropriate social and sexual behaviors, loss of awareness about changes in behavior, loss of concern about hygiene and appearance, increase in appetite that leads to constant eating and weight gain, apathy, and loss of speech and language.

Dementia with Lewy Bodies (5–10%):

Concentration problems, disorientation and other Alzheimer-like symptoms often appear first with this type of dementia. Spells of symptoms may be interspersed with periods of near-normal functioning. Later, stiffness, tremors, flexed posture, and slowness of movement may emerge. Affected individuals have a shuffling gait, reduced arm swing, and a propensity for falls. Early development of visual hallucinations is a common symptom. People may experience severe nightmares up to years prior to other symptoms emerging. Lewy body dementia is responsible for most cases of dementia in Parkinson's disease patients. If a patient develops an Alzheimer's-type syndrome and then very shortly afterward—within a year of onset—develops Parkinsonism, that is called Lewy body dementia (Rabins, Summer 2011).

Parkinson's Disease with Dementia (approximately 20–30% of people with Parkinson's disease will develop dementia):

Parkinson's disease with dementia has a similar presentation to Lewy body dementia. The symptoms are virtually the same as for dementia with Lewy bodies, except that in Parkinson's disease with dementia, problems with tremors, postural problems, and slowness will develop three to five years prior to the cognitive problems. Depression is found in 40–50% of Parkinson's patients (Rabins, Summer 2011).

Creutzfeldt - Jakob disease (CJD):

CJD is at times called a human form of mad cow disease. CJD is the most common among the types of transmissible spongiform encephalopathy found in human brains. The brain tissue develops holes and takes on a sponge-like texture. This is due to a type of infectious protein called a prion.

Subcortical Dementias: Treatable Causes of Dementia

These dementias result from dysfunction in the parts of the brain that are beneath the cortex.
Usually, the forgetfulness and language difficulties that are characteristic of cortical dementias
are not present. Rather, people with subcortical dementias display symptoms of unusual blood
pressures, blood abnormalities, stroke, disease of large blood vessels in the neck, heart valve

disease, depression, clumsiness, irritability or apathy and tend to show changes in their speed of
thinking and ability to initiate activities. The final stage of subcortical dementia is the complete
loss of brain function.

Dementia symptoms appear in a number of diseases. With proper interventions and recognized early, dementia symptoms in the following medical conditions can sometimes be reversed:

> Chronic alcohol or drug abuse
> Tumors of the brain
> Blood clots
> Normal pressure hydrocephalus
> Subdural hematoma
> Metabolic imbalances
> Hypothyroidism
> Depression
> Infection of the brain
> HIV
> Syphilis
> Urinary tract infections
> Side effects of medications
> Diseases of the thyroid, pancreas, kidney, and liver
> Nutritional deficiencies (vitamin B_{12})

Symptoms that mimic mild cognitive impairment and early Alzheimer's may result from:

- **Central nervous system and other degenerative disorders:** head injuries, brain tumors, stroke, epilepsy, Pick's disease, Parkinson's disease, Huntington's chorea.

- **Metabolic ailments:** hypothyroidism, malnutrition, vitamin deficiencies, dehydration, kidney or liver failure.
- **Substance-induced conditions:** drug interactions, medication side effects, alcohol and drug abuse.
- **Psychological factors:** dementia syndromes, depression, emotional trauma, chronic stress, psychosis, chronic sleep deprivation, delirium.
- **Infections:** meningitis, encephalitis, syphilis.

Delirium vs. Dementia: Delirium is a state of confusion which can show a number of symptoms that may mirror those found in the person suffering from dementia. There are several notable factors that will help to determine the proper diagnosis. For one, dementia is a slow process that affects memory; delirium is a fast process that affects attention. Asking several important questions regarding characteristics of delirium and dementia will help clarify the distinctions

Characteristics	Delirium	Dementia
Onset	Acute	Insidious
Course	Fluctuating	Stable
Duration	Hours to weeks	Months to years
Attention	Fluctuates	Normal
Perception	Hallucinations	Usually normal
Sleep/wake	Disrupted	Fragmented

Segment Three:
When Alzheimer's Disease Is Suspected

As was noted a number of times throughout this book, denial and minimization are two common ways we use to cope with difficult situations (especially when it comes to absorbing the plight of dementia). When we lose a boyfriend or girlfriend we say, "I didn't like her (him) anyway"; when we don't make the team we say "the coach had favorites or didn't like me." With dementia, spouses and intimate others often dismiss early symptoms of memory impairment, concentration, and confusion as isolated instances and deny the common pattern and minimize their severity.

An example of how denial may influence critical decision-making occurred recently in my practice. I was meeting with a woman who had entered the hospital following a recent auto incident. After discussing the challenges she had ahead of her, she proceeded to sob heavily, stating that she was most concerned about her husband, who had shown a number of cognitive changes over the past few months; she was worried about his being alone in their home and providing for him on a daily basis. The concerns had been "overlooked" for quite a while, she stated, and with her current situation and inability to provide for him, she now faced the reality of her husband's changes and his need for assistance in her absence. This illustrates the difficulty that families may have in identifying symptoms that may indicate Alzheimer's disease.

A definitive diagnosis of Alzheimer's disease can be made following an autopsy, when plaques and tangles can be seen. In mid-July of 2010 at an international meeting in Hawaii, experts introduced diagnostic guidelines that include brain scans to detect Alzheimer's disease before clinical symptoms of memory loss are present. These guidelines describe criteria for determining preclinical, mild cognitive impairment, and dementia phases. Under the guidelines, diagnosis will depend on **biomarkers** found in scans and spinal taps (Alzheimer's

Association 2010). Biomarkers are naturally occurring, measurable substances or conditions in the body that can be used to reliably indicate the presence or absence of disease. An example may be the level of cholesterol as a biomarker for cardiovascular disease, or blood glucose levels as biomarkers for diabetes. Research is attempting to isolate and identify the biomarkers for Alzheimer's disease. The most successful so far has been proteins in spinal fluid and brain imaging. There is new research stating that a test has been developed that will scan for plaque in the blood. This research suggests that if no plaque is found, a person will not develop Alzheimer's disease, and if plaque is found, then the potential to develop Alzheimer's increases, though without certainty.

Considering the advances in research surrounding predictive and preventive factors for Alzheimer's disease, professionals generally agree that there are six major categories requiring assessment (and periodic reassessment) for the affected loved one. They are: (a) daily function, (b) cognition, (c) co-existing medical conditions, (d) disorders of mood and emotion, (e) agitation, and (f) caregiver status.

A. **Daily Function:** The daily function criterion assesses the patient's degree of disability and dependence on a caregiver. Basic activities of daily living (ADL's), such as feeding and toileting, can be assessed with an interview or by using an assessment tool (ADL Scale). These results help with supportive planning and interventions. Activities of daily living generally include bathing, dressing, toileting, transfer, continence, and feeding. Caregivers would measure the degree of assistance necessary for each of the categories over a set time period. Each of the assessed categories is rated on a scale to provide continuing dependence levels and progress of the disease process. There are a number of other categories that may be assessed having to do with functional capabilities, such as using a telephone, traveling, preparing meals, housework, taking medications, and the like. Clearly identifying daily care difficulties will aid in caregiver education to provide the most beneficial care to the person with Alzheimer's. It will also help to reduce caregiver distress and fatigue through better preparation and anticipation of problem areas.

B. **Cognition:** Rate of cognitive decline during the course of the disease may vary due to neuronal change, co-morbid medical and social factors, and environmental adjustments. Therefore, it is important to assess and reassess when noticeable changes appear in daily functioning, affect, cognition, and critical stress times. Slippage in memory, visual and spatial skills, and language require caregivers to understand that these changes will trigger vital personal and relational adjustments. There are a number of cognitive tests available, including the St. Louis Mental Status Exam, the Mini-Mental State Exam, the Montreal Cognitive Scale, and the Clock Test. These tests assess cognitive functions, such as orientation, attention and calculation, recall, language, and the ability to copy three-dimensional designs. A total score denotes what level of cognitive loss the person has and whether dementia is present. Any assessment represents a person's functioning *at a given point in time,* and scores may vary if there are extenuating circumstances that may be affecting the patient at the moment—for example, level of fatigue, pain, an illness (e.g., urinary tract infection), or recent environmental change. Dramatic changes between test dates may indicate other conditions affecting the Alzheimer's, or another disease process.

Neuropsychological and cognitive testing provides only one type of measurement of possible decline. Direct communication with people other than the spouse is vital. This provides critical information and a wide-ranging perspective on the daily functionality and subtle changes that may be occurring in the person with dementia. Information regarding a patient's functioning from a significant other can be influenced by denial and minimization, as mentioned above. The more lucid partner is not about to easily admit that the love of so many years is mentally unstable and unsafe and may have to leave their home.

C. **Co-existing Medical Conditions:** Patients with Alzheimer's disease frequently have other medical conditions, such as cardiovascular disease, infection, pulmonary disease, renal insufficiency, arthritis, and diminution of vision and hearing. The approach one takes to treating co-existing medical conditions must take into account the phase of dementia and its effects on care planning, communication abilities, benefits and risks of treatment, and adherence to treatment. Medical treatment decisions are difficult to make, especially if the patient has extensive comprehension and/or expressive difficulties.

Blood tests are done to rule out anemia and infections, either of which can cause or complicate the dementing illness. Blood chemistry tests are used to check for kidney or liver problems or diabetes. Other medical tests include the EEG (electroencephalogram), which records the electrical activity in the brain. Advanced radiological techniques such as CT, MRI, PET, and SPECT scans can help the physician identify changes in the brain that may indicate strokes, Alzheimer's disease, and other conditions that can cause dementia. In addition, the caregiver stress associated with this disease only increase when potentially life-threatening/-saving decisions are to be made.

D. **Disorders of Mood and Emotion:** As the dementia takes over a person's life, there is a high potential for behavior problems, psychotic symptoms, anxiety, and depression. These problems are principal determinants of the need for institutionalization and a major cause of caregiver distress. These disturbing changes are generally reported by the caregiver first, and, if the behavior turns aggressive, the caregiver may be the recipient of harm. The patient must be evaluated for medication toxicity, basic communication lapses, and medical, psychiatric, psychosocial, and other environmental complexities that underlie behavioral concerns. The development of a treatment plan begins at the first interview and should be reassessed every six months to provide the best treatment and help reduce the need for a more restricted placement.

E. **Agitation:** Agitation generally increases over the course of the disease. There can be a number of triggers, including pain, medication, psychosocial stressors, and increasing cognitive decline, which causes loss of communication clarity. It is important to rule out treatable causes and iatrogenic agitation, that is, agitation occurring due to hospitalization. This is more likely in older patients with far greater frequency due to a variety of patient age-related changes, multiple chronic conditions and complexity of illness, provider lack of awareness, and education and organizational structure and process factors.

F. **Caregiver Status:** The physical and emotional health of the primary caregiver is critical to providing optimal care for the person with Alzheimer's disease. Caregivers can suffer a myriad of medical and psychological concerns directly related to the emotional and physical stress, time, and energy required to care for the patient. The key to coping with diseases of dementia is creativity and ingenuity. As the disease progresses, the affected person lives life without planning, recognition of consequences, or the ability to identify how his or her behavior affects others. Care must reflect the ability to balance the ever-changing presentation with the longer-term planning for safety. It is imperative to assess the stress levels of caregivers to reduce complicating issues that hamper care. It is healthy and quite common that counselors, social workers, and support groups operate throughout the disease continuum, for caregiver help.

Along with understanding the major categories required in the continuing assessment of Alzheimer's disease, professionals currently have a number of methods to help with a proper diagnosis. These include a detailed patient history, which gathers information regarding the type and onset of symptoms, patient and family history regarding medical and psychological conditions, and an assessment of the current living environment, including medical, social, and emotional well-being. Other important pieces of data come from family and close friends. These people can provide valuable insights into the daily behavior and personality of the affected person. Many times, a close person can tell of changes prior to the evidence shown with formal testing. As stated earlier, professionals may perform physical and neurological exams, blood and other medical tests to help determine neurological functioning and identify possible non-AD causes of dementia. Additionally, there may be a request for neuropsychological testing to test for tasks measuring memory, language skills, ability to do arithmetic, and other skills related to brain functioning to determine any changes occurring in the brain. **The greater the scope of information gathered at the onset of an evaluation, the greater the chance of properly identifying and treating the presenting concerns.**

Many times, gathering information from all aspects of a person's life is difficult, so it is very important to find competent professionals with experience in working with dementias with access to several means of diagnosing Alzheimer's disease. Most people will come into their primary care physician's office with the first complaints about their spouse or parent. With knowledgeable professionals the proper consults are then made to further determine the cause of changes and the best treatment options.

Segment Four:
The Diagnosis: Through the Phases

Let's face it. We are a frightened lot when it comes to Alzheimer's disease. Most people over 50 worry more about Alzheimer's disease than cancer, heart disease, or diabetes. Most people who are reading this book have a direct or indirect connection to the disease; either through their family, through a close friend, or by professional association. (The others probably remember me from high school and cannot believe that I could come up with something so useful!) But for the former bunch, there are questions we ask ourselves regularly—most frequently, questions related to whether we will get the disease. What are the chances? People want to know whether they carry the "genetic gifts from their family." Then there are the questions related to cure, or quality of life. Issues of protection or prevention, such as eating right and exercising the body and the brain, come up. Close behind are the questions of financial, legal, and other forms of responsibility.

People can become very skilled at hiding the initial and early-phase manifestations of cognitive decline. Sometimes it is a family member who begins to notice the changes in reasoning, understanding, or using appropriate judgment in the person with dementia. Other times the people with early symptoms are themselves the first to notice the subtle changes associated with losing words, drifting thoughts, or forgetfulness. People will respond in different ways, including concealment, lists, denial with blaming others or circumstances, or becoming increasingly depressed or cranky, or even more cheerful, disarming and distracting from the major concerns.

Alzheimer's disease is most often diagnosed by the cognitive, behavioral, and social changes that occur as the disease progresses. The debilitation associated with Alzheimer's disease advances differently for each person; some changes are more predictable than others. People with Alzheimer's differ in the patterns of problems they experience and in the speed with which their abilities deteriorate. Their abilities may change from day to day, or even within the same day. What is certain is that the person's abilities will deteriorate—sometimes rapidly over a few months; in other cases, more slowly, over a number of years.

Mild cognitive decline announces an outward change in cognitive functioning but not necessarily the beginning of dementia. Very mild cognitive decline is generally considered "age-appropriate" decline without any significant features that would raise alarm in family or close friends. Mild cognitive decline is associated with mild cognitive impairment with the beginning of clear-cut deficits. The affected person, family, and close friends all notice these not-so-subtle changes.

Moderate cognitive decline can be considered the early part of the dementia process. Now, clear losses in recent memory, serial tasking, and concentration indicate this moderate level of cognitive decline. Interactions with family and close friends are increasingly affected.

As the disease begins to affect the cerebral cortex, memory loss continues, and changes in other cognitive abilities emerge. The clinical diagnosis of Alzheimer's disease is usually made during this time. Signs can include:

- Memory loss
- Confusion about the location of familiar places (getting lost begins to occur)
- Taking longer to accomplish normal daily tasks
- Trouble handling money and paying bills

- Poor judgment leading to bad decisions
- Loss of spontaneity and sense of initiative
- Mood and personality changes, increased anxiety

The growing number of plaques and tangles first damage areas of the brain that control memory, language, and reasoning. It is not until later in the disease that physical abilities decline, and this delay can lead to a situation in which a person seems to be healthy, but is actually having more and more trouble making sense of the world around him or her. The acceptance of these often subtle and "normal" changes can be difficult to accept.

Understanding what lies ahead for the person with Alzheimer's disease and the family can certainly help to reduce the sense of panic and unpreparedness we all feel as our loved ones slip into their own world. So it remains important to:

- Pay attention to the initial warning signs
- Confirm these concerns with others who have daily or regular access to time with the person
- Become familiar with what you're are looking for— the symptoms of dementia
- Take appropriate actions with close others, identify professional resources and seek interventions at an early time
- Begin to "map out the territory"—organize your care plans into the future whenever possible
- Manage family and other caregiver stress

When Alzheimer's disease is properly diagnosed, the cognitive decline is clearly noted. If the impaired individual is living with the family or in close proximity, where they are part of the care system, the cognitive and behavioral changes are causing daily concerns and changing the daily routines of the family. There's an increase in appointments to be made, interrupted schedules, and, most importantly, *decisions about present and future care*. There is no more hiding or running from the truth. What happens during this moderate phase sets the tone and care direction until the death of the family member with dementia.

In the moderate phase, disease damage has spread further to the areas of the cerebral cortex that control language, reason, sensory processing, and conscious thought. Affected regions continue to atrophy, and signs and symptoms of the disease become more pronounced and widespread. Behavior problems, such as wandering and agitation, can occur. Increasing supervision and care become necessary, and this becomes more difficult for spouses and families.

The symptoms at this point can include:

- Increased memory loss and confusion
- Shortened attention span
- Problems recognizing friends and family members
- Difficulty with language; problems with reading, writing, working with numbers
- Difficulty recognizing thoughts and thinking logically
- Inability to learn new things or cope with new or unexpected situations
- Restlessness, agitation, anxiety, tearfulness, wandering—especially in the late afternoon or at night
- Repetitive statements or movement; occasional muscle twitches

- Hallucinations, delusions, suspiciousness or para-noia, irritability
- Loss of impulse control (shown through sloppy table manners, undressing at inappropriate times or places, or vulgar language)
- Perceptual-motor problems (a person can fall when getting out of a chair or setting a table)

Behavior is the result of complex brain processes that take place in fractions of a second in the healthy brain. In Alzheimer's disease, many of these processes are disturbed and are the basis for distressing and inappropriate behaviors. For example, a person may angrily refuse to take a shower or get dressed because he does not understand what his caregiver has asked him to do. If he does understand, he may have forgotten how to do it. The anger masks his fear and/or anxiety. The person with Alzheimer's disease may begin to follow a spouse or caregiver around the house because she is fearful and confused with the current environment, not remembering the past nor having the ability to anticipate the future. Sticking close to a trusted person is the only thing that makes sense and gives safety.

Advanced Alzheimer's dementia features severe cognitive decline accompanied by increased behavioral changes that are unpredictable and potentially dangerous. This phase of the disease brings the demented to a state of losing recognition of the family, talking incoherently, being disoriented and focused in the moment, and having only glimpses of their former life. With advanced Alzheimer's, **families begin to forget the person they knew and may not want to know the person he or she has become.** At this point, plaques and tangles are widespread in the brain and areas of the brain have atrophied further.

All illusions of potential hope are going fast in the final part of this phase. If the person with Alzheimer's is with family at home, there is 24/7 care. Otherwise, patients are placed in a skilled nursing arrangement for their and others' safety until they pass. They are dependent on others for care. All sense of self appears to vanish. Other symptom can include:

- Weight loss
- Seizures, skin infections, difficulty swallowing
- Groaning, moaning, or grunting
- Increased sleeping
- Lack of bladder and bowel control
- Calling out for help without apparent reason or recognition of doing so
- No understanding of how their behavior affects others
- Disinhibition of all behavior
- Unpredictable mood changes
- Delusions

The dementias represent a collection of disorders that describe losses in thinking, behavior, and functional areas. The onset of dementia symptoms may be temporary or permanent depending on the initial cause. With Alzheimer's disease, the symptoms are progressive and eventually will lead to death. The course of the disease varies according to a number of factors, and the effect on the family can be prolonged and overwhelming.

Chapter 5

Further Considerations

Wings of angels, tears of saints
Prayers and promises won't bring you back,
Come to me in my dreams again
Wings of angels, tears of saints

—Judy Collins, *Wings of Angels*

This chapter will present the reader with important co-existing factors that affect people with Alzheimer's disease and their care-givers. A review of the key points involving care by family members and what to expect from the loved one with Alzheimer's at the various phases will help the reader assimilate and summarize previous information and assist with providing a time-line to help identify the myriad changes in the loved one, simplify an action plan, and focus on key concepts and trends for the family.

Almost three months have elapsed since Rob passed. He suffered with Alzheimer's disease and succumbed following seven-plus years of declining health and debilitating loss of function. He developed pneumonia, which he could not fight due to his already compromised condition. His family was close and supportive to the very end. Marlene, his wife, their two daughters and a son, seven grandchildren, and four great-grandchildren, toiled through his long decline. During the initial grieving period, friends, and co-workers expressed a great deal of comfort and assistance to the family. Marlene continued to have solid support from close friends and neighbors when her children and grandchildren returned to their homes. Meals were cooked, the telephone was busy, and there were daily offers to assist. Marlene accepted some offers but also desired to spend time alone in her home so that she could grieve her loss. Evenings were the most difficult time, as she would sit alone and reflect on better times with Rob. He had not been the partner she married over the past several years, but she used his mere presence as strength for herself. Now she was truly all alone, and no matter how many people supported and comforted her, they could not possibly understand her sorrow. She became increasingly isolated and depressed. Her polite refusals to join friends for luncheon were common. She kept telephone contact with her children and their families but declined invitations to visit and spend a few days at their homes. There were legal and financial responsibilities to attend to which required timely responses, and Marlene was not able to complete some of these tasks.

The above example helps to demonstrate that the death of the person from Alzheimer's disease does not end the impact on members of the family. There are emotional highs and lows, difficulties in concentration and a general lethargy that permeates daily life.

Emotional Care-Giving

Through every phase of the disease, loved ones provide continued care and attention to their family member stricken with Alzheimer's. Early on, there are gentle reminders of names, directions to destinations, and prompts to complete daily chores. As the disease takes hold and difficulties increase, the reminders change to hands-on direction, formal cues (usually written), increased dependency of the person with Alzheimer's on caregivers who respond with increased vigilance, and growing concerns regarding personal safety and hygiene. In the advanced phase, caregivers are providing their love while recognizing they are losing the person they knew without any reward of recognition or improvement; yet they continue their vigil knowing the inevitable end.

Through each phase, the emotional toll on caregivers and family is great. Denial, minimization, guilt, and anger weigh heavily on mental and physical health. Sleep, nourishment, and concentration affect personal, social and professional lives. Many caregivers pride themselves on their ability to endure their pain and keep their stricken loved one at home. They suffer their loved one's unending repetitive questions, the increased paranoia and dependency, the doubt of their sincerity and the potential for aggressive behavior toward them or other family members. There is little rest and little recognition of the accumulating stress.

The denial that is originally expressed about the loved one having Alzheimer's disease is now denial of the toll the Alzheimer's is taking on the caregiver. In the later phase, caregivers can no longer deny their loss. Depression sets in, regrets about a life lost, fear for their future, and an extreme sense of helplessness to change the clearly marked course—and these feelings may last a significant amount of time following the loved one's passing.

Friends and *secondary* family members will be moving through their own grieving process as the disease progresses. Some will be losing a dear friend, card partner, poker buddy, fishing buddy or quilting partner, great uncle, or reliable neighbor. They will not share their grief with the immediate family for fear of upsetting them, yet they continue to suffer. For any significant person in the life of the person with Alzheimer's, the preparation for change in life is real and important. Life has changed and will continue to do so as you accommodate the loss. People grieve differently, and there is no official time or way to move through the loss. Many people discover that a spouse of a person afflicted with Alzheimer's, who has suffered for years through the slow debilitating trauma, may feel a significant relief of stress and will have begun grieving long before their loved one has passed. Others may grieve for months and even years after the passing. There is no judgment here, only the understanding that because we all grieve differently, sometimes there is an inability to share our grief and accept how another's grieving process may be different from our own.

Listening to the garbled words, yelling, or delusional speech can be very disconcerting to the family. There may be a tendency to shy away from visitation or engaging in any communication. Although research confirms the mass of tangles that occur in the brain and the harm it does to the cognitive abilities of the person suffering, there is a saying within the dementia groups: **"If you've seen one dementia patient, you've seen one dementia patient."** The message is clear. **No two people go through this disease in the *same* manner.** Two days prior to my father's passing from Alzheimer's disease, he sat in his wheelchair, looked sharply into my eyes, smiled at me, and mumbled a phrase I was not close enough to hear. He had expressed neither verbal communication nor clear direct eye contact for approximately seven months prior to that period.

Professionals are not clear what the parameters of awareness are from one moment to the next with people who suffer from Alzheimer's dementia. It is important to not disregard the person with Alzheimer's because you are not getting the response you want or the kind of recognition you long for. It is important to speak, listen, and be active in the life of the person with Alzheimer's through the time of their passing. There are those who state that it is important to talk about the life of the person suffering when they were healthy and vibrant, because when the dementia took over "they were not themselves and it was the disease talking." I agree, but having Alzheimer's disease does not define the person. *This person continues to be Joe who now has Alzheimer's disease. There is more to Joe than the disease.*

There is a period of time that family and others who have recently lost a loved one will want to avoid the emotions and general thoughts of the person whom they recently lost. At times talking about your grief can be too painful, and the tendency to not talk at all increases. Denial may work for a short period, as when the person with Alzheimer's is first diagnosed, but in the end this only prolongs the grief and misery of the loss.

Who Cares?
Considering that the "prime directive" has been the care and safety of the person with Alzheimer's, it is easy to not pay attention to the personal cost of providing that care. As noted above, the physical and mental toll can be great. Providing

time for caregivers to nourish themselves is urgent, and there is much written on self-care for those in that position. Personal boundaries are blurred and misjudged. With the intensity of care required in the advanced phase, many caregivers do not recognize the warning signs of poor health or the resources and opportunities that are available to them. Second generation caregivers (children) and third generation caregivers (grandchildren) will themselves tend to ignore, or not receive, the care they look for. Children are highly vulnerable in this regard. They are losing their grandparent and, in a sense, their parent(s) during this period. They may not be able to grieve, ask questions, or be present with members of the family as the time of death nears or the behavior of the person with Alzheimer's makes it dangerous or inappropriate for them to spend time together. The extent of the disengagement of family members from one another may last a significant amount of time following the death of their loved one and, without recognition and discussion of how the family system has changed, could cause irreparable damage to the relationships.

There are numerous books, articles, seminars, and support groups dedicated to primary caregivers and their families. The mental and physical toll can be devastating if the caregivers do not care for themselves. The bibliography that follows the final chapter in this book will guide the reader to several resources, and I *strongly* encourage all readers to develop a support system.

Alzheimer's Disease and Pain

As the disease progresses, the expression of pain will vary. Pain can be expressed through verbal, nonverbal, and facial expression. Early in the disease process, it is important to establish a baseline of how you measure pain. Self-reporting is the single most reliable indicator of pain, and so it is urgent to determine the most dependable method of attaining the correct information.

With mild cognitive impairment and through the early to moderate phase, people with Alzheimer's can inform others about their pain, locating and describing it with ample information to help get the proper treatment. They can answer questions regarding when the pain started, whether they have had similar pain before and, probably, what helped. They know whom to address to identify the general treatment possibilities and whether they are feeling better following attention to the pain. As their vocabulary decreases and words become more difficult to find, caregivers may hear statements like "I took those little pills, the ones in a box like that." Specificity declines and vague responses begin to offer little help in identifying and alleviating the problem pain. During this transition time, caregivers must begin to pay increasing attention to other signs of pain and be able to understand the *distorting* expressions provided by the person suffering.

As the person with Alzheimer's moves further through the moderate and advanced phases of the disease, the clinicians and caregivers must rely on behavioral cues. The pain signals vary from individual to individual as the disease progresses. As the affected person loses expressiveness, the onset of pain can cause her to become highly agitated and combative. Intimate others and facility staff that have knowledge and pay attention to the pain indicators generally have an easier time with care and stability of the affected loved one. Failure to recognize and treat pain adequately can lead to malnutrition, sleep disturbance, decreased mobility, and unnecessary placement in a skilled nursing facility (Smith and Buckwalter 2005). Crying, moaning, and groaning sounds often can signal pain, as can sudden withdrawal from social activities and family, increased confusion, resistance to care, restlessness, and rubbing certain parts of the body.

Pain assessment should occur during different times during the day and evening, when the affected loved one is resting or engaged in varying levels of the daily routine. This will help establish a baseline and help to clarify times of pain. Pain management includes verbal, behavioral, and pharmacologic interventions that should be developed by the treatment team. The team should include family, if appropriate; facility or home staff familiar with the person with Alzheimer's general functioning; and the medical doctor and other professionals who may give pertinent input regarding the loved one's functioning.

When the Primary Caregiver Cannot Care for the Person with Alzheimer's

Considering that up to 95 percent of people who develop Alzheimer's disease are 65 years old or older, it would be highly likely that caregivers of the same generation would have their own medical and/or mental health problems. The stress of providing daily care will exacerbate any ongoing conditions caregivers have and may even contribute to the decline of their general health. With more time and energy spent as caregivers, fatigue and poor self-care may follow. The need for relief from providing care to a loved one due to ill health may lead to guilt and depression. If the person with Alzheimer's is living with the primary caregiver and can no longer count on that person's assistance, she may have to leave their home or other stable environment and suffer a downward spiral in functioning. This, in turn, would cause continuing negative self-reflection for the caregiver. During these difficult times a caregiver should give serious thought to having *respite care*. This opportunity provides for another caregiver to come to the home, or for temporary placement of the affected loved one in a safe environment, providing the primary caregiver time off from their care-giving responsibilities. Respite care providers can generally be found through contact with a physician, primary care facilities or the local branch of the Alzheimer's Association.

Hospice

Hospice services are designed to support individuals at the end of life. Services may include support groups, visiting nurses, pain management, and home care. Hospice services are usually arranged through the treating physician; they are usually not available until the physician anticipates that a person has less than six months to live. Having hospice enter the situation is not an automatic forecast of impending death. I have worked with many people afflicted with Alzheimer's disease and co-existing medical problems who, while receiving hospice care, regained strength and general fitness and were removed from hospice care. Crucial decisions for holders of POA and family members arise with end of life care when other medical concerns are present. Decisions to treat problems such as: infections, hospitalizations, blood transfusions, surgery (emergent or elective), dialysis and fractures can cause high stress. It is wise to seek advice from professionals who can help sort out viable solutions to this highly charged issue. There are several questions the family could consider regarding hospice involvement:

1. Had Advanced Directives been established earlier when the person with Alzheimer's was able to take an active part in the decision-making process?

2. Has there been adequate research and discussion with professionals to determine that hospice is the appropriate course of action at the present time?

3. How will the decision to use hospice now affect continuing life decisions for the affected loved one (e.g. how to deal with poor eating or pain)?

4. Is the family ready to work through the potential emotional discord that end of life decisions can present?

5. Will the family be ready to work through the post-passing emotions that will arise in family members who felt strongly about a different course of action?

6. If the family decides to continue with hospice care, what criteria will they use to modify or change that agreed-upon decision if necessary?

Guidelines for family when the loved one begins life in a facility:

Do your research about the facility to make sure this is the proper place for your loved one
Set up your loved one's room simply and, as far as possible, similarly to previous residence

Put your loved one's name or a familiar object on the door

Develop a routine for scheduled events

Use your loved one's name; talk slowly, using few words

Use photos or gestures to help clarify what you want (hold up the glass to check if the loved one is thirsty)

Understand the policy for family visits and for the loved one's time out of the facility for home visits or meals if this is appropriate

Find out who the medical doctors and other professionals are, and how to communicate with them

Designate someone to be the main contact person for your loved one

Be aware that the move to another environment will probably cause an increase in confusion in your loved one, hopefully only temporarily

Let the staff at the facility do their job. Be a visitor with love and compassion.

Key Points for Family Care:

Throughout the book there have been generic case examples of how Alzheimer's disease affects family systems. While each family situation has unique elements, there are central focal points of care for those with Alzheimer's disease. This segment illustrates, by phase, the more common difficulties and continuing abilities of the person with Alzheimer's, how the personal and social lives of teens and children may be altered, and what parents can offer to assist them through their adjustments.

Mild Cognitive Impairment (MCI)

Changes in the person with MCI:
*   Has difficulty that is evident to intimates in finding words and names

- May forget names upon introduction to new folks
- May misplace or lose valuable objects
- Is increasingly distracted, forgetful, restless
- Exhibits loss of attention

Continuing abilities for the person with MCI during this time include:
- Awareness of simple errors; ability to correct them
- Reliance on routine for independence
- Using a sample to learn a new task
- Working with two concepts or tasks together (ironing and listening to the radio)
- Completing self-care in familiar environments
- Completing simple home management
- Walking and driving in a familiar locale without getting lost
- Reading and using information in small amounts
- Orientation to time, place, and situation

During this time the relationships between teens, children, and the person with MCI remain constant, with little change in routine, safety, recognition, and overall satisfaction, although extensive time and travel with children could tire the affected person.

- Satisfying relationships are maintained
- Roles are clear
- The person with MCI remains a positive and a helpful role model
- There appear to be no safety concerns with travel or time together
- The grandparent with MCI and the grandchildren continue to enjoy and look forward to time together

As with children and teens, the entire family continues to operate as though there are no concerns, and interactions are respectful, with role clarity. Specifically:

- Families continue to respect their loved one's independence
- There is a "business as usual" approach to relationships
- Families generally do not pay attention to "minor mistakes"
- With family not paying attention to the minor cognitive changes, there are the missed opportunities to discuss potential medical and/or legal intervention

Early Phase Alzheimer's Dementia

Throughout this phase, the person with early phase dementia exhibits subtle but increasingly common and noticeable decline. Specific changes noticed in the person with early phase dementia include:

- Getting lost traveling to unfamiliar locations
- Poor performance at work
- Trouble learning and retaining new information
- Increased denial of problems
- Forgetting where familiar objects are placed
- Change in nutrition and tastes
- Forgetting names of those formerly known well
- Growing suspiciousness and blaming
- Trouble making choices or handling money
- Responding to direct questions with vague explanations
- Questionable safety risk awareness

- Increase in apathy and isolation from the family
- Repeating phrases, stories, or questions in same conversation
- Losing track of time and responsibilities during the day
- Problems with personal hygiene and self-care concerns
- Increase in forgetfulness and loss of attention to specifics
- Exaggerated (emotional) responses and mood changes
- Concentration deficits noticed with formal testing
- Increased denial and minimizing of family concerns

The daily functioning level and ability to perform tasks varies only slightly during the course of the early phase. Much of what the person with early phase dementia could complete during higher cognitive functioning remains intact. The changes are the *frequency of events* that are associated with dementia, and the family's growing alertness to the situations. Toward the end of the early phase, greater assistance is necessary to help the affected person maintain a semi-independent lifestyle. Increased family intervention and growing dependency of the person with Alzheimer's on the family provides the clear indication that their loved one is entering a new phase of the disease.

The person with early phase dementia functions best when presented with the same cueing and assistance as provided during milder cognitive impairment. The transition to diagnosable dementia may incline people with Alzheimer's to resist care, as it requires them to acknowledge obvious loss and dependency needs. With family members, the transition could exacerbate already existing dynamics that preclude acknowledging the initial onset of Alzheimer's. This could cause the rejection of care from the family's side, thus increasing danger for the affected person.

An important key to success involves the ongoing open communication within the family and the inclusion of professionals who could more clearly explain to the person with Alzheimer's the changes they are experiencing and how the family could aid them.

Relationships with grandchildren begin to change due to the noted decline in the person with early phase Alzheimer's. Specifically:

- There may be increased mistakes concerning expected care for dependent younger grandchildren
- Younger grandchildren may giggle at verbal or behavioral errors, and the grandparent may cover with humor
- The affected person may begin to withdraw from "over-stimulating" times or challenging tasks or games with grandchildren
- Younger grandchildren may withdraw from or lose patience with their grandparent
- Children may express an increase in physical pain (such as stomachaches or headaches) as a way to cope with increasing family strain
- Children and teens may show a drop in their schoolwork if the grandparent lives in their home and is showing noticeable changes
- Teens note and comment on forgetfulness; they may lose patience, find fault, and correct mistakes

- Children and teens begin to ask parents about the changes they notice in their grandmother or grandfather
- At times children and teens may appear embarrassed by the grandparent's behavior; they may not feel comfortable having friends over to the house
- Teens may not want to talk with their friends about the changes going on in the home
- If the grandmother or grandfather lives with the family, the child may miss out on care and attention from their parents or be asked to take on other jobs and responsibilities.

Family interactions begin to show signs of stress, and concurrently there are usually feelings of closeness and growing interdependence among the members. Specifically:

- All members of the family notice patterns of change in the grandparent
- Initial role-changes (reversals) over complex day-to-day tasks between parent and adult child
- If the grandparent lives with family, the level of frustration and intolerance may grow with increased complaints by all members of the family; routines are changing
- When children help out with their grandparent, they feel like the family really needs them
- Children could feel closer to their parents as everyone in the family is going through this difficult period together

There is an increased need for safety precautions in situations when the person with Alzheimer's is left in charge as the responsible adult; backup plans are advised regarding the affected person's completion of deadlines and of daily responsibilities. Several general guidelines would help:

- Maintain clear boundaries and role identity for all members of the household (e.g. not having the grandchildren "*paren*"' their grandparent)
- Identify the tough situations for family members
- Minimize secrets
- Maintain appropriate active family involvement
- Plan early
- Anticipate the need for help, and get it when needed
- Become familiar with the facts about Alzheimer's disease and the effects on all involved
- Investigate and plan for the professional resources the family will need in the future

MODERATE PHASE ALZHEIMER'S DEMENTIA

During this phase of the disease, vast changes occur in the person with Alzheimer's and family. Some of the major changes include:

- The person with Alzheimer's requires daily assistance and should not live alone
- The person with Alzheimer's cannot reliably recall many significant details of her or his life during an interview—phone number, address, grandchildren's names, etc.
- There is frequent disorientation to date, day, week, number sequencing, etc.
- Making choices becomes more difficult—selecting clothes, restaurants, etc.
- There is lowered tolerance for environmental stimulation and associated higher confusion
- Sleeping habits may change
- The person with moderate dementia's personal boundaries become poor (decision-making, judgment, insight to own condition)
- Other medical conditions become a larger factor in care-giving; the person with dementia may exhibit resistance to seeing physicians or visiting a medical office
- Hygiene issues arise (daily cleanliness, oral hygiene, changing clothes)

- The person with dementia may experience loss of fluent speech, word loss, and aphasia
- The family member with Alzheimer's may experience delusions, which can cause increased dependency and shadowing of care-givers

Due to deteriorating abilities caused by moderate phase Alzheimer's, there is fallout for the affected grandparent's relationship with grandchildren. If the grandparent lives with the family, some of these effects are:
- Younger grandchildren may become highly disturbed by the erratic and unpredictable behaviors, language, and thought processes expressed by their grandparent; this may make them more cautious and possibly fearful
- Grandchildren's behavior patterns may change with increased stress:
  o School grades may drop or the child may not complete homework assignments
  o Sleep patterns could change, including increased restlessness and nightmares
  o Relationships may change with friends as the grandchildren and their parents may not want others to observe the behavior of the grandparent
- Younger children will tend to spend less time with their grandparent
- Teens will tend to spend less time in their home
- If teens are called upon to take on care-giving responsibilities, they may feel resentment towards their grandparent and family
- Children and teens will ask more questions regarding the changes in their grandparent

- Children and teens may engage in behaviors (e.g. isolation) or make comments (e.g. "We don't do anything because of Grandma") that will reflect the increased emotional changes in the family environment

Some of the activities that can help to keep the relationship between the grandchildren and grandparent positive include:
- Baking cookies
- Taking walks around the neighborhood
- Working on puzzles
- Weeding and planting in the garden
- Drawing or coloring
- Scrapbooking, organizing photos
- Reading a favorite book
- Having picnics
- Watching television together
- Listening to and singing familiar songs

Family transitions during this phase are enormous. The grown son or daughter of a parent with Alzheimer's may be hosting both parents and having to parent two sets of dependents. It is during the latter part of this phase that strong consideration is given to having the parent reside in a more structured environment. Some family considerations include:
- Addition of in-home care for the parent as behavior and confusion require increased personal attention
- Paying close attention to possible increased guilt regarding the need to spend time caring for the parent and consequent decreased attention to other family members

- Loss of available time for family interaction, vacations, and leisure
- Reprioritizing daily chores due to the degree of care necessary for the parent
- With considerations for having the parent move to a more restricted environment, primary family and relatives begin to "weigh in" on decision-making
- Safety and medical concerns other than Alzheimer's begin to have a greater effect on the general health of the parent
- At this phase, if hospitalized with a medical condition, the parent has a greater possibility of not returning to the home upon discharge
- Caregiver stress becomes a growing factor that has secondary effects on other family members, especially children
- Family communication with professionals from the medical, mental health and legal fields becomes essential for maintaining best care practices for the affected loved one.
- The family member with Alzheimer's will maintain stability and identity with activities that involve reminiscing and anchoring.

Advanced Phase Alzheimer's Dementia

Entering the final phase of the disease, people with Alzheimer's have a fragile sense of "selfness"; they know who they are but cannot recount details of their life; they can identify most significant people in their life but cannot recall their names or what their relationship is; they can identify many utensils they handle and how to use them, but will not call them by name; they will recognize some familiar locations when they are there, but not know why they are there or how they got there. In this phase attention span is sporadic and for less than a minute. They will see an object in their walking path but be unable to respond quickly enough to go around it; they may bump into it or ignore and try to walk through it. If the person with advanced dementia survives to the end stage of the disease, then the most basic abilities will continue to exist.

Major changes include:
- Loss of ability to correctly identify others; the person with dementia may call an individual by someone else's name
- Significant unawareness of recent life events
- Distortion of time and sequencing in some memory of personal history
- Gross misuse of words and "word salad"; over time, complete loss of speech is not uncommon, with only utterances and occasional words or phrases making sense
- Incontinence (bowel and bladder) becomes the norm through the phase
- Sleep cycles are inconsistent
- Changes in environment cause confusion
- Frequent onset of delusions, primarily of paranoia
- Fixation on items in the environment, and compulsive behavior
- High potential for anxiety and aggressive behavior (usually reactive) due to confusion and fear
- Increased disinhibition; the person with dementia may strike out without provocation

- Cognitive abulia (loss of will power) because the person with dementia cannot carry thoughts long enough to find purpose
- Basic psychomotor skills lost; losing ability to walk; generalized rigidity

Child and teen interaction will now take place at the skilled nursing facility or other restricted residence in which their grandparent resides. It is important for parents to prepare their children for visiting their grandparent in this contained environment. There will be other residents who exhibit similar behaviors and appear with medical conditions that may be disturbing to the children. Several key considerations for their visits include:

- Ask children and teens if they want to visit their grandparent. Do not force them if they prefer not to. Help them explore their reservations with understanding from their perspective.
- Considering that their grandparent may recognize but not be able to correctly identify who they are or how they know them, younger children can be very upset and not understand how "Poppie could forget who I am."
- Expect that children and teens could have highly emotional responses, which may be displaced onto other people or situations (e.g., an older child picking a fight with a younger sib as a way to release emotion).
- Children should be asked to bring something to share with their grandparent when visiting their new residence; drawings and objects belonging to Grandma given by the grandchild are examples.

- Following each and especially the first visit, parents should be available to discuss feelings, thoughts, and observations with children and teens.
- While teens may decide not to participate with visits to see their grandparent, younger children are bound by their dependence on parents' schedules. Parents must balance their desire to be with their parent with the level of discomfort of their child and with their role as mother or father.
- Comments by teens may appear callous and uncaring concerning the charged situation and their displaced emotions can affect their highly sensitive parents and cause unnecessary strife.

A final thought regarding children, teens and Alzheimer's disease

By taking the time to understand how a child or teenager is feeling and talking to them about the disease, you can support their adjustment to the changes they are witnessing. It is important to reassure children and teens that you are still there for them, and that you understand the difficulties they face. They need to know that, despite all the pressures, you still love them – however preoccupied or snappish you may seem at times. Make sure you have regular quality time, when you can talk without interruption. Use reassurance, and clearly explain the reasons why their grandparent became ill. Very young children may need reminding why the person is behaving in a strange way, and all young people will probably need to talk about their feelings as new changes develop.

There is no easy way for children and teens to accommodate the changes and loss of a close loving grandparent. As parents, we have a responsibility to guide them through the loss in a caring, nurturing, and dignified manner so that their memories capture the whole person. Alzheimer's disease may ultimately take the life of our loved family member, but not the loved one's place in our family.

Adult family members are preparing for their loss. As the disease takes its final toll on their loved one, decisions become necessary surrounding issues of continuing care and, eventually, resuscitation efforts. Specifically, the effects of such transitions may play out as follows:

1. The initial decision to have the parent placed in a long-term care facility could cause extensive guilt and remorse.

2. Most caregivers will not be satisfied with the care received at the skilled facilities, as it is not at the level of attention and intimacy provided at home.

3. A new major adjustment to lives of all family members is stressful and demanding. Scheduling children, work, and care meetings can rattle even the most calm and efficient family systems.

4. Communication between families and skilled facilities can be slow, with less satisfying information to the family because of the number of people involved in decision-making (specialists, medical and nursing personnel, social workers, therapists, and the number of patients with whom the professionals are working.

5. It is wise for the family to decide who will be the lead contact person to receive information from the skilled facility and other professionals.

6. The potential for guilt regarding questions of maintaining life increases when their loved one cannot provide any self-care.

7. *Do not ask the affected loved one if they know your or others' names; tell them who you are; use statements, and limit your questions*

At this phase, the person with dementia functions best with:

1. Consistent, predictable schedules

2. Reduced visual and auditory distraction

3. Visual or auditory cues to start familiar tasks

4. One-step tasks only

5. Enough time to talk themselves through tasks

6. Verbal or/and physical assistance to help with completion even of simple tasks

7. Family members speaking very slow, use few words, and if possible, making direct eye contact before verbally communicating

8. Supervision for safety

* * *

The information presented in this book reflects knowledge gathered by resources throughout the medical, scientific, and mental health fields. Even as this book goes to publication, research continues to provide newer critical information and hope for the millions affected by Alzheimer's disease. With continuing strides in research and supportive planning of Alzheimer's disease, professionals are working to create an environment with a goal of keeping the family system a viable and valuable resource for our loved ones. Advances utilizing medical biomarkers can help to identify those at high-risk years before the symptoms first appear. New medications may inhibit the progress of symptoms, hopefully slowing debilitating effects and helping affected loved ones remain with their families for longer periods. There is no comparable substitute for the family who provides the safe, attentive, loving, and compassionate care for affected loved ones stricken by this insidious disease. Creating an environment that can compensate for the continuing losses of a person with dementia through knowledgeable and preventive care, will positively impact the life of the person with Alzheimer's and their family and, help defray many of the costs associated with in-patient care.

In writing this book, my goals have been: to provide understanding of how Alzheimer's disease affects the functional life of the person afflicted and their family, to present *best care* interventions for the care-giving family, and to suggest how the family can create an environment that is safe for the person with Alzheimer's disease and for children and grandchildren. I wanted to illustrate situations and pose central questions that would help families utilize appropriate resources. Those of us who are the most passionate about caring for our loved ones are the most vulnerable to suffering the effects of poor self-care as we tend to their needs. Alzheimer's disease has a strong connection to aging, and with a large segment of our population reaching the ages when the disease is most likely to appear, it is imperative to recognize how we can minimize stress and reduce associated burdens. Again, there is no comparison with or substitute for the strength and spirit of family care. Remember, the gift you give in caring for loved ones comes from the gift you get from caring for yourself.

References

Books:

Alzheimer's Association (2009). *Just for Kids & Teens: Helping You Understand Alzheimer's Disease.* Chicago: Alzheimer's Association National Office. Retrieved from http://www.alz.org/living_with_alzheimers_just_for_kids_and_teens.asp.

Alzheimer's Association (2010). International Conference on Alzheimer's Disease (ICAD), July 10–15, Honolulu, Hawaii.

Gruetzner, H. (2001). *Alzheimer's: A Caregiver's Guide and Sourcebook.* John Wiley & Sons.

Kakugawa, F. H. (2002). *Mosaic Moon: Caregiving Through Poetry Easing the Burden of Alzheimer's Disease.* Watermark Publishing.

Long, C. (2006). *Palliative Care for Advanced Dementia: Guidelines and Standards.* Alzheimer's Association, Desert Southwest Chapter.

Mace, N. L., and P. V. Rabins (1999). *The 36-Hour Day.* 3rd ed. Baltimore: Johns Hopkins University Press.

Kakugawa, Francis H. (2002). *Mosaic Moon; Caregivning Through Poetry easing the Burden of Alzheimer's Disease.* Honolulu, Hawaii: Watermark Publishing.

Zeisel, J. (2010). *I'm Still Here: A New Philosophy of Alzheimer's Care.* New York: Avery (Penguin Group USA).

Journals and Other Sources:

Alzheimer's Association, Desert Southwest Chapter Newsletter. (This publication sends subscribers quarterly newsletters four to five pages long, with articles and updates.)

Alzheimer's Association (2011). Helping Children Understand the Disease. www.alz.org/national/documents/brochure_childrenteens.pdf.

Alzheimer's Disease Education and Referral Center (2001). Progress Report on Alzheimer's Disease: Taking the Next Steps (NIH Publication No. 00-4859). Alzheimer's Disease Education and Referral Center, Silver Spring, MD.

Brandt, Jason (2011, November 2). **How Parkinson's Disease Causes Cognitive Changes.** *Johns Hopkins Bulletins,* Johns Hopkins Medicine.

Cognitive Dementia and Memory Service (CDAMS) Clinic. Wayne, M., M.A., Segal J, Ph.D. April 2009, National institute of health 2002

Cummings, J. L., J. C. Frank, D. Cherry, N. D. Kohatsu, B. Kemp, L. Hewey, and B. Mittman (2002, June 1). **Guidelines for Managing Alzheimer's Disease: Part 1.** *American Family Physician.*

Evans, D. A., et al. (1989). **Prevalence of Alzheimer's Disease in a Community Population of Older Persons: Higher Than**

Previously Noted. *Journal of the American Medical Association* 262 (18): 2551–6.

Folstein, M. F., S. E. Folstein, P. R. McHugh (1975). **"Mini-mental State": MMSE (Mini Mental Status Exam), a Practical Method for Grading the Cognitive State of Patients for the Clinician.** *Journal of Psychiatric Research* 12 (3): 189–98.

Kennard, Christine (2006). **Did Dr. Alzheimer Discover Alzheimer's Disease?** About.com, updated July 31, 2006.

Max, W. **The Economic Impact of Alzheimer's Disease.** *Neurology* 1993 (suppl. 4): S6–S10.

Peter V. Rabins, Editor. (2011, Fall). *Johns Hopkins Bulletins: Memory Disorders.* (This is a series of essays on different topics from the editor.)

———. (Summer 2011). *The Johns Hopkins Bulletins*: Memory Disorders.
———. (Winter 2011). *The Johns Hopkins Bulletins*: Memory Disorders.
———. (Spring 2012). *The Johns Hopkins Bulletins*: Memory Disorders.

Reisberg, B.(1988). Functional Assessment Staging (FAST). *Psychopharmacology Bulletin* 24: 65–9.

Reisberg, B., S. H. Ferris, M. J. de Leon, T. Crook. (1982). **The Global Deterioration Scale for Assessment of Primary Degenerative Dementia.** *American Journal of Psychiatry* 139: 1136–9.

Reisberg, B., M. K. Schenk, and S. H. Ferris (1988). **The Brief Cognitive Rating Scale (BCRS): Findings in Primary Degenerative Dementia (PDD)**. *Psychopharmacological Bulletin* 24 (4): 629–636.

Rosenberg, Paul B. (2011 Spring). **Johns Hopkins Medicine, Johns Hopkins Bulletins Memory Disorders.**

Smith, Marianne, and Kathleen Buckwalter (2005). **Behaviors Associated With Dementia.** *American Journal of Nursing* 105 (7).

Sunderland, T., et al. (1989). **Clock Drawing in Alzheimer's Disease: A Novel Measure of Dementia Severity.** *Journal of the American Geriatrics Society* 37: 725–9.

Tariq, S. H., N. Tumosa, J. T. Chibnall, H. M. Perry III, and J. E. Morley (2006). **St. Louis Mental Status Exam (SLUMS).** *American Journal of Geriatric Psychiatry* 14: 900–910.

Weiss, Barry D. (2009, June). **Frontotemporal Dementia. Elder Care: A Resource for Providers.** Donald W. Reynolds Foundation, Arizona Geriatric Education Center, and Arizona Center on Aging.

Yassa, M.A., A.T. Mattfeld, S.M. Stark, C.E.L. Stark (2011). **Age-related Memory Deficits Linked to Circuit-specific Disruptions in the Hippocampus.** *Proceedings of the National Academy of Sciences USA* 108(21): 8873–8.

Zeisel, J., J. Hyde, S. Levikoff (1994). **Best Practices: An Environment-Behavior (E-B) Model for Alzheimer Special Care Units.** *American Journal of Alzheimer's Care & Research* 9 (2).

Music CD

Collins, Judy (1999). Wings of Angels. Universal Music Corp. (ASCAP), Wildflower Company (ASCAP); produced by Judy Collins, recorded live at Wolf Trap Performing Arts Center.

Websites:

www.alz.org Alzheimer's Association

www.alzfdn.org Alzheimer's Foundation of America

www.helpguide.org/elder/respitecare.htm
Information regarding respite care

www.caremangers.org National Association of Professional Geriatric Care Managers

www.caps4caregivers.org Children of Aging Parents

www.caregiver.org Family Caregiver Alliance

www.nfcares.org Family Caregivers Association

prabins@memorybulletin.com Johns Hopkins Bulletins

www.johnhopkinsmedicine.org/rabins alzheimer's
Johns Hopkins Research Center for Alzheimer's

www.alz.org/library The National Alzheimer's Organization Virtual Library

www.agenet.com Aging Resource Network

www.aoadhhs.gov Administration on Aging

www.nia.nih.gov/Alzheimer's Alzheimer's Disease Education and Referral Center

www.nia.nih.gov National Institute on Aging

www.nih.gov National Institute of Health

www.Mayoclinic.com/health/alzheimer's/HQ00216

www.alz.org/living_with_alzheimer's_just_for_kids_and_teens.asp

www.caregiving.com Care-giving Online

Suggested Reading for Children:

Alzheimer's Association (2009). *Grandpa, Do You Know Who I Am?* New York: Alzheimer's Association National Office.

Bahr, M. (1992). *The Memory Box.* Morton Grove: A. Whitman.

Gerdner, L. A. (2008). *Grandfather's Story Cloth.* Walnut Creek, CA: Shen's Books.

Shriver, M., and Speidel, illustrator (2004). *What's Happening to Grandpa?* Little, Brown Books for Young Readers.

Garrigat, M. M. (2011). *Sarah, the Little Fairy: Grandma Gets Lost!* Sanoen.

Made in the USA
San Bernardino, CA
19 November 2015